MYTHS OF THE ZODIAC

MYTHS OF THE ZODIAC

Hugh Lloyd-Jones

sculptures by

Marcelle Quinton

DUCKWORTH

First published in 1978 by
Gerald Duckworth & Co. Ltd.
The Old Piano Factory
43 Gloucester Crescent, London NW1

© 1978 by Hugh Lloyd-Jones and Marcelle Quinton

ISBN 0 7156 1096 1

British Library Cataloguing in Publication Data

Lloyd-Jones, Hugh
    Myths of the zodiac.
    1. Zodiac
    I. Title   II. Quinton, Marcelle
    133.5'2   BF1726
    ISBN 0-7156-1096-1

Photographs by Don Honeyman
Filmset and printed in Great Britain by
BAS Printers Limited, Over Wallop, Hampshire

Preface

The sculptures which illustrate this book aim at astronomical accuracy; they have regard for the positions of the stars which make up each constellation of the Zodiac. Some of these constellations resemble the persons or things they are named after more closely than do others. The names are mnemonics, coined to help the observer to recognise the constellation. Some are visual, like Scorpio; some are suited to the season at which the sun passes through the sign in question, like Aries; some are both visual and seasonal, like Leo.

The introduction sketches the history of the Zodiac. Whatever one may feel about astrology, it has played and still plays a considerable part in human history; and this sketch takes account of its importance.

The myths by which the Greeks explained the names given to the signs are narrated in versions taken from the Greek and Roman poets. If some of these seem unfamiliar, it may be because they are based on poems preserved in papyri found in Egypt and published only in recent times.

H.Ll.-J.
M.Q.

Contents

Introduction

The sun's annual path through the heavens—and we still speak of his path, even though we know that it is the earth that moves—can be marked by a line defined by various groups of stars that lie along it. This line is known as the Ecliptic, because eclipses happen only when sun and moon are both situated upon it. Sun, moon and planets confine their movements to a narrow band some 8° to either side of the Ecliptic, which is called the Zodiac. The Zodiac derives its name from a Greek word meaning 'living creatures', from the same root as the word from which we derive 'zoo'; and it is so called because each of the twelve sections of 30° each into which it is divided is named after a constellation falling more or less within that section. Most of these constellations are named after persons or animals, whose shape they are fancied to resemble. Most of the resemblances between stars or constellations and the objects they are named after appear to be extremely far-fetched; the first names were a rough aid to memory, useful to sailors and to farmers. The names we use for the signs of the Zodiac are those used by the Greeks; a verse gives them in their astronomical order:

> The Ram, the Bull, the Heavenly Twins,
> And next the Crab the Lion shines,
> The Virgin and the Scales,
> The Scorpion, Archer and He-Goat,
> The man who holds the Water-Pot,
> And Fish with glittering tails.

A more succinct mnemonic runs:

> Ram, Bull, Twins, Crab, Liverish,
> Scaly Scorpions are good Water-Fish.

But this requires us to remember that the Virgin is sometimes identified with the Syrian goddess Ishtar.

Myths of the Zodiac

Each of these names is a great deal older than the concept of the Zodiac itself, which seems not to be older than the fifth century B.C.

Egyptian astronomy goes back as early as the third millennium B.C.; but it was a comparatively crude affair, whose main achievements were the calendar which made the year consist of 12 months of 30 days each with 5 days added at the end and the day divided into 24 hours. The Egyptians named certain stars and certain constellations; in some cases their names coincided with the later names. Far more important was the astronomy of Babylon. The earliest Babylonian record we possess is that of the dates of the consecutive first and last appearances of Venus as evening star and as morning star between about 1645 and 1625 B.C.; the much fuller records known as 'astronomical diaries', preserved on clay tablets, start early in the seventh century and end during the first century B.C. Observations had been made from a much earlier date; but their phenomenal accuracy, like the phenomenal brightness of the Babylonian sky, has been shown to be a legend. Only for the last three centuries of the period covered by the texts do they reveal an astronomy based on a consistent mathematical theory of the movement of the moon and planets. The astronomy of Babylon, like that of Greece, reached a high scientific level only during the late fifth century B.C.

How far Babylonian astronomy influenced the Greeks is a disputed question. Early Greek philosophers from the beginning of the sixth century are often alleged to have known something of Babylonian observation of the sky. Yet for Thales of Miletus to have predicted an eclipse, as he is said to have done in about 585 B.C., he would need to have made use of the results of a technique not developed till three centuries later. The evidence is vague, and the interaction between the two astronomies is impossible to document with certainty; some still believe there was a parallel development, but it seems far likelier that there was some connection.

The greatest living authority on ancient science, Otto Neugebauer, thinks the Zodiac was a Babylonian invention. The earliest Babylonian text to mention it is a horoscope dated to 410 B.C.; the division of the Ecliptic into twelve equal signs is mentioned in another Babylonian text of the early fifth century. The Greeks ascribed the discovery of the Ecliptic to Oenopides of Chios, who lived about the middle of that century; the Greeks knew of the Zodiac during the last third of it, when Meton and Euctemon were laying the foundations of a scientific astronomy.

Introduction

The Zodiac had a place in the system of the greatest Greek astronomer of the fourth century, Eudoxus of Cnidus, a friend of Plato. His system was in harmony with the physics of his younger contemporary Aristotle; Eudoxus' own distinctive contribution was the doctrine of concentric moving spheres. At the centre of the system was the globe of earth; above the earth, an envelope of thick and dark atmosphere reached as far as the moon. Beyond the moon were the successive spheres of the sun and five planets; Mars, Jupiter and Saturn were above the sun, Venus and Mercury below; last came the eighth sphere, composed of heavenly fire, the purest of material elements, and containing the fixed stars. In this universe the humblest portion was the earth, the domain of chance, mutability and death.

It was the system of Eudoxus that was described in verse by the great poet Aratus (315–240 B.C.); he was the court poet of Antigonus Gonatas, King of Macedonia, and like him a member of the Stoic sect of philosophers. Hipparchus (*c.* 194–112 B.C.), the great astronomer of the second century, gave his main work for convenience's sake the form of a commentary on the poem of Aratus. It was Hipparchus who discovered the precession of the equinoxes; the points where the ecliptic cuts the equator move slowly but steadily westward, so that in the course of centuries the stars visible in a given locality change considerably. Thus the point of the spring equinox, which in Hipparchus' time was in the sign of the Ram, is now in that of the Fish; but many astrologers have blandly continued to act as though the zodiacal constellations had not altered their positions since the Hellenistic age.

Some of the Zodiacal signs were called by the Greeks by names taken over from the Babylonians—the Twins, the Lion, the Fish, the Bull, the Scorpion. The Ram, the Crab, the Water-Pourer they called by different names; in the case of the Maiden, the Archer and the Goat, the names have not been proved to be the same. This state of affairs seems perfectly consonant with the Babylonian origin of the Greek Zodiac; one would expect some names to be altered, but most names to be preserved. It is remarkable that the Babylonian astronomers refer to the 'horn', or as we say the 'claws', of the Scorpion by the name of Scales; after the time of Hipparchus, the Greeks increased the number of the signs to twelve by cutting off the claws of the Scorpion and calling them the Scales. Most, perhaps all, of these names of constellations are older than the Zodiac itself.

Myths of the Zodiac

The practical importance to sailors and farmers of observation of the heavens is very great. It was inevitable that they should carefully observe certain prominent stars and constellations, and that they should designate them by means of their resemblance to familiar and therefore easily memorable objects. Observation of the stars of a more systematic kind was indispensable for the creation of a calendar, which seems to have happened first in Egypt.

It was natural for the Greeks to see the persons or animals after which they named the stars in terms of their own religion and mythology. The Homeric epics, dating in their present form probably from the eighth century B.C; contain several names of stars and constellations of this kind (Pleiades, Hyades, Bear or Wagon, Orion and his dog). Hesiod's *Works and Days*, probably not much later, is a manual for farmers; since it often indicates when a particular task should be carried out, it contains a greater number of such allusions, naming much the same stars as Homer. The earliest known manual of astronomy was in verse and was ascribed to Hesiod; it was probably as early as the seventh century. It was not the only such poem. We have scraps of an astronomical poem by Cleostratus of Tenedos, a writer of the sixth century. Poetry was connected with astronomy long before the great astronomical poets of the third century B.C., and its contribution to the naming of the stars must have been extensive. But the stars became important in religion in a way very different from their importance in mythology.

In Babylon the early religion had developed without regard to astronomy. The gods of sun and moon and the goddess Ishtar, who was identified with the planet Venus, were not without importance, but they were not at first predominant. But the observation of the heavens by the priestly caste led to the invention of a new star religion. The regularity of the movements of the heavenly bodies led the Babylonians to the notion of a fate or necessity determining the lives of men, and even of the gods themselves. They held the universe to be eternal, and since when the stars resumed a former position all must happen as before, they held history to consist of a succession of vast cosmic cycles. Nietzsche imagined that he had invented the doctrine of the eternal return; but it is present already in the religion of the Babylonians. They worshipped not only the sun and moon, but the five planets and all the constellations of the firmament. The planets were identified with the great gods; Marduk corresponds with Jupiter, Ninib with Saturn, Nergal with Mars, Nebo with Mercury, as well as Ishtar with Venus. Once they had adopted the concept of the Zodiac, it was natural for them to assume that a man's fate depended upon the sign through which the sun was passing at the moment of his birth. Each sign of the Zodiac occupied thirty degrees of the 360° of the Zodiacal circle; each was divided into three sections of ten degrees, each presided over by a separate divinity called a decan, a notion which derived from Egyptian astronomy.

In Greece the worship of the heavenly bodies was not a native feature of religion. The sun and moon counted, like other powers of nature, as divinities, but only as very minor ones; the identification of sun and moon with Apollo and Artemis is very rare indeed till well after the classical period, and when the sun had an important cult, as he did in Rhodes, for instance, it happened because of foreign influence.

Yet Greek philosophy from its beginnings tended to regard the heavenly bodies as divine. This happened partly because the philosophers were impressed by the regularity of the movements of the stars, but partly through the influence of the religions of the neighbouring oriental countries. Plato recommended that the heavenly bodies should be worshipped; and the dialogue *Epinomis*, ascribed to him but probably written by his pupil Philip of Opus, seconds the recommendation in a way that clearly shows the influence of Babylonian star-worship. Yet in the fourth century, when this dialogue was written, star-worship had not yet taken root among the Greeks; Eudoxus explicitly rejected it. Only after Alexander's conquests had broken down the barriers that separated them from the oriental world did they become a prey to it.

During the third dynasty B.C. the doors of Greek philosophy were opened to astral religion by the Stoics, whose founder, Zeno of Citium in Cyprus, began to teach in Athens in about 300. His oriental origin is almost certainly not significant; the genesis of the Stoic philosophy can be explained without difficulty in terms of Greek antecedents. From Plato the Stoics took over the belief that ideal excellence resides in undiluted form in a higher world than ours. Divine reason, according to the Stoics, controlled all things; it resided in that very ethereal fire of which the stars, in the universe presented by Eudoxus, consisted. The parts of the universe were united by a cosmic sympathy; but they were not all of equal value: the human soul, a tiny

13

particle of the ethereal fire, was all that was truly good in the world beneath the moon. Divine reason determined all things, so that every event in the universe was predetermined and could in theory be predicted; the stars above constituted 'the army of unalterable law'. The heliocentric theory put forward during the third century by Aristarchus of Samos did not suit the Stoic universe; the Stoics used their influence to kill it, and it disappeared until Copernicus revived it.

Stoic determinism and Babylonian star-worship were natural allies; and now that the way was clear for direct and regular intercourse between Greece and Babylon, the alliance could be open and official. During the third century, a Babylonian priest, Berossus, wrote in Greek an account of Babylonian history and religion; during the second Diogenes of Babylon became head of the Stoic school, and Archidemus founded a Stoic academy in Babylon itself. Not all Stoics surrendered to astral religion; the great Panaetius (*c.* 185–109) had no use for it. But in the next generation the most important Stoic philosopher was Posidonius of Apamea (135–51), a man of genius who did much to humanise the grim rigour of the Stoic discipline. In his work on divination in five books, Posidonius accepted the possibility of prophecy; and though the details of the lost work remain uncertain, it is clear that his powerful influence was favourable to belief in the religion of the stars.

After the Persian conquest of Egypt during the sixth century, Babylonian star religion had become closely linked with the indigenous religion of that country. In the Ptolemaic kingdom established by the Greeks during the fourth century, an astrological literature written in Greek but made out of Babylonian, Egyptian and Greek elements came into being. The Egyptian god Thoth, identified with Hermes Trismegistus, 'the thrice-greatest Hermes', figured as the revealer of wisdom to men; so did the Greek Asclepius and the Egyptian Anubis. The sacred texts of the new religion were the mystic treatises attributed to the legendary Egyptian king Nechepso and his friend the priest Petosiris; they existed before 150 B.C., and presented not simply a method of divination but a religion, partly derived from Greek philosophy. The so-called Hermetic books, compiled between 50 B.C. and A.D. 150, contain a complete theology which spread rapidly throughout the Roman world. In Syria the religion of the local Baalim took on a new aspect under the influence of Babylonian astral doctrine.

Introduction

Many educated Romans of the Republican period, like Cato in the second century B.C. and Cicero in the first, resisted astrology. But the early centuries of the empire saw many different religions established at Rome itself and all over Rome's dominions; most of these acquired a link with astral doctrines. The mysteries of Dionysus; the mysteries of the Egyptian goddess Isis; the cult of the Greco-Egyptian divinity Serapis; the Persian cult of Mithras; all these took on an admixture of astrological belief. So did the revived Pythagoreanism which now became an influential philosophy; belief in astral determinism was by no means confined to uneducated or semi-educated persons. The astral religion knew how to make itself acceptable to the authorities. The comet seen at Julius Caesar's death in 44 B.C. was identified with Caesar's star. Virgil imagined the celestial Scorpion drawing in its claws to make room beside it for Augustus. The Pantheon at Rome, built by Augustus' right-hand man Agrippa, has in its dome a picture of the heavens based upon an astrological conception. Claudius in A.D. 52 tried to expel the astrologers, but it was useless. The great astronomer Ptolemy, presenting under the Antonines the picture of the universe, founded on the work of Aristotle and the Hellenistic astronomers, that was to retain authority all through the Middle Ages, by reason of his astrological beliefs mingled with his scientific matter much that has no securer basis than popular superstition. After the end of the Antonine dynasty in the late second century A.D., the moment from which Gibbon starts his account of the decline and fall of the Roman empire, the link between the emperors and astral religion became official. The emperor was identified with the Unconquerable Sun; what the sun was in the heavens, the emperor was on earth. Septimius Severus married a member of the family of the hereditary high priests of the Sun at Emesa, in Syria; her great-nephew Heliogabalus, succeeding to the empire, actually tried to subordinate the whole pantheon of Rome to the black stone which represented this somewhat eccentric local divinity. His attempt failed; yet fifty years later, Aurelian, conqueror of the Syrian queen Zenobia and builder of the first city walls Rome thought it necessary to build for her protection, officially promoted the Unconquerable Sun to the first place in the imperial hierarchy. The great third-century philosopher Plotinus stood out against astrology; lesser Neoplatonists were more accommodating. From now on pagan religion was permeated by it, and the last pagan emperor, Julian the Apostate, was a convinced believer in its doctrines. The dynasty which produced the first Christian emperor, Constantine the Great, had started by having a special relationship with the Sun cult, and even after that emperor's conversion traces of the link survived.

Astral religion laid the strongest emphasis upon the eternity of the heavenly bodies. Time, or Eternity itself, was worshipped as the First Cause, a doctrine that seems to have originated with a Persian sect. 'Eternal' was a common epithet of Heaven, which was worshipped as the greatest of the gods. Each planet and each star, and above all the sun, was thought to be divine; and great veneration was accorded to the Zodiacal constellations. The vast mass of astrological writings is full of descriptions of their properties, and the monuments of pagan worship, especially those pertaining to the cult of Mithras, are covered with their images. Not only the twelve constellations that gave their names to the signs but also the thirty-six decans received this treatment. The influence of the signs, resulting partly from the mythical character of their symbols, but often from their astrological properties, was particularly powerful during the month over which each presided; and individuals paid special attention to their own birth-signs. Events on earth might be affected by the action of spirits, or 'demons'; but their power was purely local. Unlike theirs, the influence of the heavenly bodies was effective everywhere; it was *catholic*, a useful term which modern religion has taken over from astrology.

Christians who have understood their religion properly have at all times been opposed to astrology. It involves worshipping the creation instead of the creator, and its determinism undermines that free will which is essential to the Christian view of human life. Yet Christianity is so closely linked with Hellenistic and Oriental religion, philosophy and science that it was bound to overlap at certain points with astral religion; and during the early centuries of the Church many Christians in practice made some kind of compromise with its pervasive doctrines. From an early date we find Christ identified with the Sun of Righteousness, the Light of the World; these titles, familiar to us from a Victorian hymn and a Victorian painting, take us back to the world of star religion. It is because of star religion that our day of rest is the day of the sun, and not Saturday, the Jewish Sabbath; it is because of star religion that we celebrate Christ's birthday on 25 December, the birthday of the Unconquerable Sun before Christ took it over. A Christian

Introduction

might argue that though the stars moved only in accordance with God's will they might still offer signs to men; had not the Star of Bethlehem guided the wise men to the manger where Christ was to be born? In vain St Augustine placed in the fifth book of the *City of God* the most powerful refutation of astrology that has come down to us from antiquity, strengthening and supplementing the arguments of Hellenistic philosophers; in vain the emperor Justinian anathematised those who believed, as even the great father of the Church Origen had believed, that sun, moon and stars were sentient powers.

In the eastern half of the empire astrology had always been firmly established, and when Byzantine culture revived after the dark age of the seventh and eighth centuries, it was comfortably ensconced. The late-ninth-century emperor Theophilus set up a chair of it at Constantinople; the twelfth-century emperor Manuel Comnenus studied it keenly, and blinded a monk who had launched a reasoned attack on it. During the last centuries of the empire the flood of astrological literature became vast; even before the empire fell in 1453 it had been pouring into western Europe.

The rigidly deterministic view adopted by Mohammed ensured that Islam would provide fertile soil for the astrologers. There is an extensive astrological literature in Arabic, much of it based on Greek material. Just at the time when the Byzantine emperor Theophilus was endowing a chair of astrology in the imperial city (785), the Caliph Al-Mahdi was appointing to a similar position a Greek who bore the same name as the Greek emperor. Avicenna in the early eleventh century and Maimonides in the late twelfth resisted the astrologers; so did the great historian Ibn Khaldun at the end of the thirteenth. But the movement of enlightenment set in motion by Averroes (d. 1198) regarded it as a legitimate branch of science; in thirteenth-century England the brilliant experimental scientist Roger Bacon suffered imprisonment for having traced the origin of Christianity to the conjunction of the planet Jupiter. The Arabs developed certain astrological doctrines of their own, in particular the notion that certain conjunctions of the planets, particularly Saturn, Jupiter and Mars, were grave warnings from on high.

As a result of the Crusades the strong interest in astrology felt in the East spread to the West. Contact with the Arabs led to a revival of interest in Aristotle, and with Aristotle came Ptolemy. The Hohenstaufen emperors were believers; Frederick II employed as court astrologer Michael Scott,

17

who translated Aristotle and is mentioned in the *Divine Comedy*, as well as in his fellow-tribesman's *Lay of the Last Minstrel*. During the Hellenistic age astrology had spread to India; now the Arabs made known in Europe the eastern colouring it had assumed. Thomas Aquinas went as far as to allow that physique, gender and individual character might be determined by the stars; not only Averroism, but also the neoplatonising philosophy of men like Robert Grosseteste, Chancellor of Oxford University in the thirteenth century, regarded astrology as a serious science.

Humanism at first only strengthened astrology, which had been so powerful during late antiquity. Petrarch may mock astrologers, but he is not immune from their beliefs. The Florentine Platonists Ficino and Pico della Mirandola rejected divination from the stars; but their philosophy was deeply imbued with astral mysticism. Early in the sixteenth century, a Pope as enlightened as Leo X founded a chair of astrology at Rome; similar chairs existed at Bologna, Padua and Paris. How much astrological beliefs affected the symbolism of Renaissance art has only in modern times come to be appreciated. The reformed religion was not immune against astrology. Luther and Calvin, it is true, condemned it, but Luther's follower Melanchthon publicly expounded it and strongly believed in it; in 1524 even Luther believed that an alarming conjunction of planets in the sign of Pisces must be a divine warning. Elizabeth I patronised the astrologer John Dee. Shakespeare is full of astrological allusions. During the seventeenth century, the astrological writings of William Lilly were popular in England. At the birth of Louis XIV J. B. Morin, the court astrologer, was stationed in the royal bedchamber that he might take note of the exact moment of the birth; in 1661 this person published his *Astrologia Gallica*, dedicated to Jesus Christ. The great astronomers Regiomontanus, Copernicus, Galileo and Kepler all acted to some extent as practical astrologers; they could hardly have avoided it. Even when Leibniz was directing the Prussian Academy about the beginning of the eighteenth century, the calendar of that institution predicted the weather from the planets and its astronomers cast horoscopes for princes.

Yet by his invention of the telescope Galileo had struck astrology a deadly blow; as more stars and constellations became visible, the comparative clarity and simplicity of the picture of the heavens was much reduced. Earlier astrologers had managed to survive such disasters as the discovery of the

Introduction

precession of the equinoxes by Hipparchus in the second century B.C. and the revival by Copernicus of the theory that the world goes round the sun; but now instead of seven Pleiads there were about forty, and instead of seven planets there were nine, to say nothing of some 500 planetoids. Even apart from the development of astronomic science, the climate of the Enlightenment was bound to be unfavourable to the astrologers. With the support of Louis XIV, the French *philosophes* attacked them, Bayle, Fontenelle and Voltaire in particular. During the age of reason their credit sank very low; and though they were more kindly treated by some of the Romantics than they had been by their harder-headed predecessors, the nineteenth century saw them make no effective recovery among the intellectually respectable reaches of society. But as superstitions will, astrology lived on, aided by the spread of literacy or semi-literacy.

Among educated persons it cannot be said that the astrologers have effectively recovered. But educated persons form only a minority; and during the nineteenth century astrology enjoyed an astonishing revival among the semi-educated, whose numbers were now starting to increase rapidly. In England the astrological almanacs of Zadkiel and Raphael sold in large numbers. New astrological methods were devised, incorporating the planets Uranus, discovered in 1781, and Neptune, discovered in 1846. Some set out to show how astrology fitted in with biblical prophecies and promises; others combined it with chiromancy; the signs of the Zodiac were linked with the twelve tribes of Israel. Madame Blavatsky, who founded the Theosophical Society in 1875, linked astrology with belief in re-incarnation in the Indian manner. For her, each star had a soul; her disciple Annie Besant was more moderate, believing this only of the planets. Late in the century began the proliferation of astrological periodicals, which has never ceased.

Just before the First World War Zadkiel's Almanac was selling 200,000 copies a year, and the war did nothing to make astrology less popular. The Germans, always learned and methodical, developed psychological astrology, astro-biology and cosmo-biology; impressive statistics were produced which were alleged to prove the truth of astrological prediction. American experts profited by German learning and carried its conclusions further; vastly complicated theories were developed, claiming to take account of modern astronomical discovery. Modern pundits often speak with contempt of traditional astrology, finding it no less embarrassing than some modern clergymen find traditional Christianity. Jung undertook to investigate the possible link between astrology and psychology; he was cautious, but astrologers made some play with his investigations. He was also interested in the phenomenon of 'synchronicity', which he defined as 'a psychically conditioned relativity of space and time', and which he thought amounted to a non-causal combination of events. This encouraged an Australian astrologist to argue that planets may send waves through the ether, so that we may speak of 'astro-causation' between them and human beings.

In Arizona, the Institute of Abstract Science teaches astrology 'as a branch of mathematics'. In London there is a Faculty of Astrological Studies (not part of London University); it issues certificates and diplomas, binding its graduates to observe a strict ethical code. In the United States there are at least 5,000 practising astrologers, whose customers number at least ten million. Popular newspapers in England and America have their astrological columns, which operate with a very elementary astrology, based on the birth sign only. For the advanced student there are astrological periodicals of varying levels of sophistication, besides the books and pamphlets which are everywhere on sale. During the last few years, when the uneducated have become richer and more powerful than ever before in English history, the increase in the popularity of such literature has been phenomenal.

Hardly less than the seven planets, the twelve signs of the Zodiac played a central part in ancient astrology. They were classified in many different ways, so that the influence of the stars on human character and fate could be determined. The mythical associations of the signs were one consideration, but not a particularly important one. Six signs counted as masculine and six as feminine; this division is based not on gender, but on the Pythagorean notion that odd numbers are masculine and even numbers feminine. Some signs belong to day, others to night; some are fruitful, some barren, some neutral in this respect; some are running, some standing, some sitting, some lying. Each has one of the twelve principal gods for its guardian. Some are bestial, some human figures; their character will affect that of the human beings born while the sun is passing through one of them. The signs are divided into three groups of four, each one of which is associated with a different season, a different age of man, a different element, a different wind, a different physical quality, a different degree of consistency. The medical

Introduction

theory of the humours becomes linked with the four groups of signs; each group corresponds with a different fluid (blood, bile, black bile, slime), a different temperament (sanguine, choleric, melancholy, phlegmatic), a different colour (red, yellow, black, white). Just so animals, plants, precious stones and metals are associated with the signs, as with the seven planets. A whole system of astral meteorology and a whole science of astral medicine rested upon these notions; plagues were thought to be caused by emanations from the stars, and the word *influenza*, the Italian for 'influence', is a memorial to this belief. The parts of the human body were related to the signs, according to a system often depicted on old calendars. Some doctors never operated on any part of the body while the moon was in the sign associated with that part, for fear the moon's moisture might cause rheumatism or inflammation; some never gave a purgative while Jupiter was in conjunction with the moon, for fear that that planet's well-tempered nature might destroy the purgative's effect. The ailments of a given part of the body were best treated by a plant or herb under the same planet or the same sign as itself, or as the day on which it had become afflicted. By taking this way of thinking even further, the possibilities of prediction could be, and were, very widely extended; and when astrologers employed not only the planets and the signs, but also other stars north and south of them, the possibilities in question were almost infinitely multiplied.

More complicated, and more important, than the properties of the signs were the geometrical configurations that were thought to reveal the full significance of their positions. If we inscribe in the circle of the zodiac four equilateral triangles, each angle falling upon a different sign, we obtain four groups of three signs each; if we inscribe three squares, we obtain three groups of four signs each; if we inscribe two hexagons, we obtain two groups of six; certain common qualities are attributed to the members of the groups thus created. If we draw six lines through the centre of the circle, the signs we find directly opposed to one another stand in a special relationship; so do the signs linked by parallel lines drawn across a diameter of the circle. Friendships and enmities exist between the signs, and these are significant in predicting what will happen. Different planets have their houses in different signs; the sun and moon have only one house each, but each of the other five planets has two houses, and each planet has its exaltation—the moment when its power is greatest—in one particular degree of a particular sign, and its depression—the moment when its influence is feeblest—in another. Different degrees of each sign belong to different planets; these are called the terms. Each ten degrees of the Zodiac belong to a different god; these thirty-six gods are called decans, and seem to have originated in Egyptian astrology. Houses, exaltations and depressions, terms and decans all serve to link the planets with the Zodiac.

To cast a person's horoscope, or to forecast the success or failure of an undertaking, you must know the exact moment of the person's birth—or, as some astrologers preferred, his conception—or the exact moment at which the undertaking will begin. You must then discover the part or degree of the Ecliptic which stands at the part of the sky which is rising in the east over the horizon at the moment in question; originally you had to know which star was rising, but the degrees of the Ecliptic furnish a more precise method of calculation.

A proper astrologer had not only to observe the heavens, but to use his globe, circle and astronomical tables. The circle of the Zodiac was divided by four points (in Latin *cardines*) into four quadrants. The eastern quadrant contained the degree of the Ecliptic that marked the vital moment; that degree was called the ascendant. Originally the term *horoscope* denoted that eastern quadrant; later it was applied to the entire *thema*, the position of the stars at the decisive moment. The ascendant determined three other points, one in each of the remaining three quadrants. One, the *occasus*, was in the west; another, the *medium caelum*, was in the north; a third, the *imum caelum*, was in the south. The ascendant determines also the twelve *loci, templa* or houses; each of the four quadrants divides into three of them. The houses and the aspects of life which each determines are as follows:

1. Horoscope	the entire course of life
2. The Gate of Hell	possession and profit
3. The Goddess	brothers and sisters
4. *Medium caelum*	parents
5. Good Fortune	children
6. Bad Fortune	health and sickness
7. *Occasus*	marriage
8. Death	death and legacies
9. The God (the Sun)	religion, travels

Introduction

10. *Imum caelum*	home, country, honours, skills, character, mode of life
11. Good genius	benefits, friends
12. Evil genius	enemies, captivity

This is only a very summary account of the factors that must be taken into consideration; the ingenuity of the astrologers over the ages has thought out innumerable complexities.

The dominance exercised over men's minds for countless centuries by astrological belief is a most startling phenomenon. Curiosity about the future and the love of classification are not by themselves sufficient to account for it. In the eighth chapter of his famous book *The Greeks and the Irrational*, E. R. Dodds has discussed the reasons for the decline of Greek rationalism and the rise of astral determinism and other forms of dogmatism during the Hellenistic age; that chapter is entitled 'The Fear of Freedom'. 'For a century or more the individual had been face to face with his own intellectual freedom,' he writes, 'and now he turned tail and bolted from the horrid prospect—better the rigid determinism of the astrological Fate than that terrifying burden of daily responsibility.' Rational men, he adds, tried to check the retreat by argument; but without perceptible effect; 'certain motives are beyond the reach of argument'.

THE SIGNS

I. Aries

The Ram   March 21 to April 20

Beneath the belt of Andromeda one makes out the Ram; none of his stars exceeds the third magnitude. Their resemblance to a ram is by no means obvious. We cannot be certain that the early Babylonians saw them thus; but the Ram was known to Cleostratus of Tenedos late in the sixth century. For us he is the leader of the Zodiac, but not for any Greek before the Hellenistic age. Eudoxus in the fourth century begins the Zodiac with the lion, and Callippus in the third with the crab. Geminus in the first century B.C. is the first Greek authority who beyond doubt started with the Ram, and even after his time some did otherwise. The truth is that astronomers did not particularly care which Zodiacal sign came first; astrologers, however, did. Greco-Egyptian astrologers put the ram first, perhaps after a Babylonian precedent; since his rising marks the beginning of spring, he was not a bad choice for this position. The Egyptians may have favoured him because they were familiar with the ram-headed god Ammon, worshipped at the great oasis of Siwa in the Libyan desert. The Greeks identified this god with Zeus, and greatly respected his famous oracle. Alexander the Great paid him a visit, and learned here that his true father was not Philip of Macedon, but the god Ammon himself. One story actually identifies the zodiacal Ram with one which led the army of the god Dionysus, on his way to conquer India, to the oasis.

The Ram is sometimes shown leaping, and with head bent back; at other times he is jumping through a hoop sitting facing back over his shoulder. His tutelary goddess is Minerva, doubtless by association with his neighbour Perseus; it was Minerva, or Athene, who helped Perseus to bring back the head of the Gorgon Medusa. Perseus himself, his wife Andromeda, her father Cepheus and the head of the Gorgon are all found in the sky not far from the Ram. According to Virgil, the Ram was shining in the sky when the Greek fleet sailing back after the fall of Troy was rounding the promontory of Caphereus, in the south of Euboea, where there are some of the most dangerous rocks in the whole Mediterranean. If any of the heroes noticed this, he may have guessed that danger lay ahead; for Athene was angry with

27

the Greeks because of sacrilege against her temple committed during the sack of Troy, and as they sailed round Caphereus a terrible storm came upon them.

Almost all good authorities identify the celestial Ram with the ram who saved Phrixus and Helle from their wicked step-mother, the same ram in quest of whose golden fleece Jason and his crew of heroes sailed in the ship Argo to the distant land of Colchis.

Boeotia, the marshy part of Greece north of Attica, was once ruled over by a king called Athamas, son of Aeolus. He ruled over the eastern part of Boeotia, bordering on the sea, with his capital at Orchomenos; here until the present century was the great Copaic Marsh, now drained by modern engineers. His subjects belonged to a people called the Minyae, a people also living in Thessaly, to the north; Iolkos, now Volos, was the capital of another son of Aeolus.

Athamas had a wife called Nephele; the word means 'cloud', and Nephele was a cloud, a supernatural being. After the common fashion of divine wives married to mortal husbands, Nephele vanished, leaving Athamas with two children, the boy Phrixus and the girl Helle. As his second wife, Athamas married Ino, a daughter of Cadmus, founder and first king of Thebes, a little to the west. She was the child of a divine mother, Harmonia, daughter of Aphrodite.

Cadmus had come to Thebes from his father's kingdom of Tyre, far away on the Phoenician coast. He had come searching for his sister Europa, who had mysteriously disappeared (see p. 36). Cadmus never found her, but instead settled down in Thebes. By his immortal wife he had four daughters. One of these, Semele, was secretly visited by Zeus himself. This came to the notice of his august consort, Hera, who as so often felt bitter pangs of jealousy. Changing herself into the likeness of a chattering old woman, she approached the beautiful Semele. She encouraged her to boast of the attentions of her all-powerful lover; then she suggested that Zeus could not have appeared to Semele in the form he took when he consorted with his legitimate wife. Falling into the trap, Semele persuaded Zeus to promise to grant her a favour; when he had promised, she demanded that he should approach her in the same form in which he approached Hera. In vain Zeus warned her of the danger; but he could not break his promise. Semele was unable to survive contact with her lover in his natural form; already

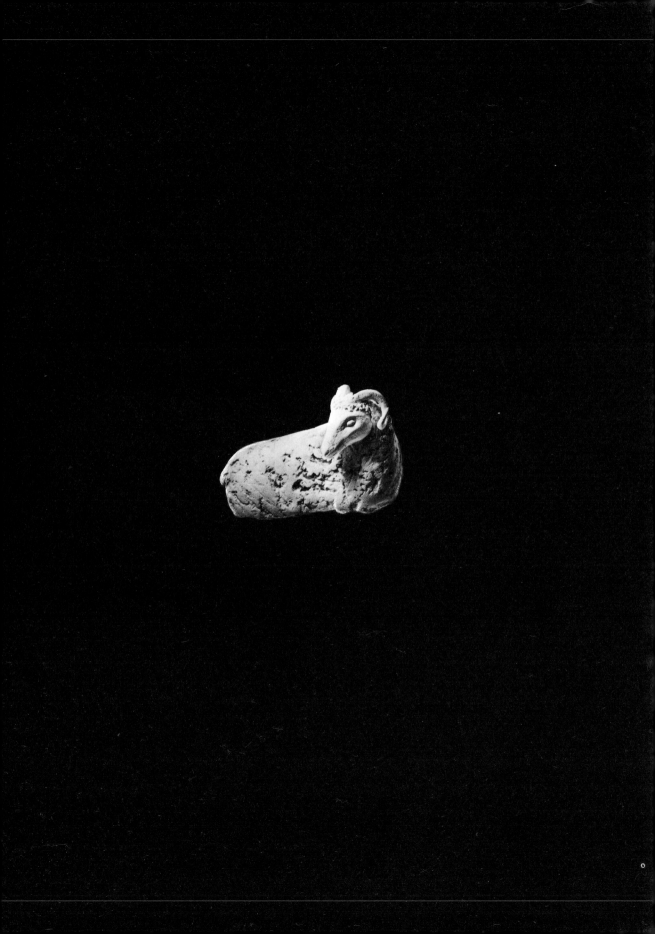

pregnant, she was consumed to ashes. As she expired, Hera sent her messenger, Iris, the goddess of the rainbow, to destroy the infant. A famous vase in Berkeley, California, shows her, sword in hand, looking angrily for the child. But she is too late; Hermes, the messenger of Zeus, has moved a split second before her, and has the child safe in his arms. He took the infant to his father, who sewed it into his own capacious thigh until it should be ready to be born. So it came about that the great god Dionysus, also called Bacchus, had two births.

Very different stories are told of the behaviour of Semele's three sisters, Ino, Autonoe and Agaue, to the mother of Dionysus and her divine offspring. Some say that her sisters, and particularly Ino, nursed the child tenderly and helped to guard him from the pursuit of the malevolent Hera. But others say that they were jealous of their sister, and even accused her of having tried to safeguard her reputation by impudently claiming Zeus as the father of her love-child. If the second story were true, it would help to explain the misfortunes of Ino, which were so great that they became proverbial; if the first were true, it would help to explain their final happy ending.

Like many step-mothers Ino became fiercely jealous of her step-children Phrixus and Helle, who seemed to stand in the way of her own two sons by Athamas, Learchus and Melicertes. To incriminate them she devised a fiendish scheme. Just before it was time to sow the corn-seed in the fields, Ino roasted the seed, making sure that the corn would not grow. When the crop failed, Athamas did what any Greek ruler would have done in such a case; he sent an envoy to Delphi to ask Apollo's oracle for advice. Ino bribed the envoy, and he told the king that the oracle had declared that the corn would grow only if he sacrificed his children by Nephele. This is not the only legend that suggests that in early times human sacrifices were not unknown in Greece; Artemis sent winds to detain the Greek fleet at Aulis on its way to Troy until Agamemnon should have sacrificed his daughter, Iphigenia.

Athamas was horrified by such an appalling order; but like Agamemnon he could not refuse to obey what seemed to be a divine command, and to apply the only remedy against famine. Phrixus and Helle, wearing the wreaths usually placed upon the heads of sacrificial victims, were led to the altar, in the presence of a sorrowing crowd. But just as the dreadful preparations for the sacrifice were complete, a strange cloud appeared in the sky, and rapidly descended over the group around the altar. Phrixus and Helle found themselves taken by the hand and led inside the cloud, which swiftly disappeared from sight. Inside the cloud they found a strange companion, a great ram whose fleece shone like bright gold. They mounted on the ram's back; the cloud carried them to the sea and there descended; and the ram carrying the two children stepped from the cloud and swam rapidly away from the Boeotian shore. Let no one persuade you that the ram flew through the air; all the earliest evidence for the story, which comes not from books but from works of art, tells us that he swam, and so do the best authorities among the poets.

The ram carried the two children right across the Aegean Sea, and all the time they managed to maintain their grip. But when they came to the narrow passage between Europe and Asia that is now called the Dardanelles, Helle, exhausted no doubt by the long voyage, relaxed for a fatal moment her hold upon the golden ram's horn. Phrixus desperately tried to save his sister, and almost shared her fate. But the ram carried him through the Dardanelles and the Sea of Marmara all the way into the Black Sea, till it finally stopped at the mysterious country on its northern coast sometimes called Aeea, but better known as Colchis. Helle gave her name to the Dardanelles, which the ancients called the Hellespont. At the first appearance of Russia in western literature we find Colchis ruled by a king not notably more sympathetic than Ivan the Terrible or Joseph Stalin. Aeetes was no ordinary human ruler; he was a brother of Circe, the immortal enchantress who bewitched the crew of Odysseus, and their father was the Sun-God, Helios, himself. But Nephele had influence with powerful gods, and a divine message warned Aeetes that Phrixus must not be treated badly. He gave him in marriage a daughter of his own, Chalciope, and with her Phrixus lived happily at Colchis for the remainder of his life.

But what happened to the ram? Phrixus was commanded to sacrifice him to Zeus, and his golden fleece, which had magical properties, was suspended in a sacred grove and guarded by a dragon. To modern minds Phrixus seems guilty of ingratitude to his preserver; but this is not how the ancients thought of the matter. The ram was no ordinary animal, but a magic creature specially manufactured by Zeus to serve his purpose; and in any case he was richly rewarded for his services, for in the end Zeus gave him the special honour of a place in heaven.

But the ram's importance did not end with his death or his catasterism. To continue with the history of the golden fleece, we must move back across the Aegean to Iolkos, in Thessaly, the home of the northern branch of the Minyae, ruled over by the brothers of Athamas, Cretheus and Salmoneus.

Salmoneus had a daughter of supreme beauty; because of her milk-white complexion she was called Tyro, a name deriving from the word for 'cheese'. One day while she was bathing in the rapid river Enipeus, the river god caught sight of her and sprang upon her. But just as he was on the point of having his way with her, he was disturbed by a formidable competitor. No god was more powerful in Thessaly than Zeus' brother Poseidon; it was he who with his trident cleft the great mass of mountains separating Olympus to the north from Ossa to the south so that the mighty river Peneus, which rises in the great range of Pindus to the west, could pour out into the sea. Strong as he was, the river god could not stand up against the Earth-shaker, and Poseidon took Tyro for himself. But her stern father Salmoneus would not believe that her seducer had been a god; and when she gave birth to twin sons, she was obliged to expose them in the woods.

As the two infants lay helpless on the ground, a herd of wild horses passed perilously by them. The hoof of a mare struck the face of one of the children, leaving a livid mark, that led to his being named Pelias, from a word that means 'livid'; his brother was named Neleus. The injured child's cry attracted the attention of the herdsman driving the horses, who took the infants home and reared them.

Meanwhile Salmoneus, following a custom not unusual even in historical times among the Greeks, had given Tyro in marriage to his brother Cretheus. By that marriage she had three sons, Aeson, Pheres and Amythaon, all destined to have illustrious sons. But later Cretheus took another wife, Sidero, whose name rightly suggests that she was hard as iron. She persecuted the unfortunate Tyro, cutting off her wonderful hair, spoiling her matchless complexion, and condemning her to a life of servitude.

Just as Tyro was about to perish at the hands of her persecutor, who with her armed attendants had come to the remote place in the country where Tyro was confined, her two sons, now grown to manhood, made their appearance. Sent to draw water at the well, Tyro encountered them and they recognised each other. Sidero's guards outnumbered the opposition, but they were no match for the two sons of Poseidon. Sidero fled to the altar of the goddess Hera, knowing that if she could manage to get there in time the solemn law that forbade the killing of suppliants would protect her. Just as she touched the altar, the sword of Pelias cut her down. That made Hera a deadly enemy of Pelias to the last.

After that Pelias, very naturally, took the throne; his brother Neleus made his way to Pylos, in the south-west of the Peloponnese, where he reigned as king. He married Chloris, the only one of Niobe's children to survive their massacre by Artemis and Apollo. Chloris' own sons were equally unfortunate. All perished in a battle against the mightiest of all heroes, Heracles; one only was absent at the time and so survived, and that was Nestor, who lived to be the oldest and wisest of the Greek chiefs who besieged Troy.

Aeson, the son of Tyro by Cretheus, was pushed aside from the succession; and when his son was born, for fear of his half-brother Pelias he smuggled him out of the town to the cave on Mount Pelion where the wise Centaur Chiron educated the sons of heroes (see p. 84). When he had reached fighting age, the boy Jason made his way to the city of Iolkos to claim his heritage from his formidable uncle. On the way he came to a mountain torrent in full spate, and as he was preparing to cross it, an old woman appeared and begged him to carry her across. With heroic courtesy, Jason complied; as he was struggling across the river, one of his shoes was carried away. The old woman was none other than Hera in disguise; her gratitude to Jason was reinforced, if reinforcement was needed.

An oracle had warned Pelias to beware of the man with one shoe; so that when he drove up in his chariot and saw the people in the market-place admiring the splendid appearance of the young hero, he knew he was in danger. The detail of the shoe is significant; according to the earliest legal procedure the heir to a property formally asserted his right by taking off a shoe in order to set his bare foot upon the ground that he was claiming.

Pelias asked Jason his name and origin in tones of arrogant contempt; but Jason, always prudent, answered calmly and politely, pretending not to recognise the king. He had come, he said, to claim his inheritance, of which the unjust Pelias had cheated him. Instead of challenging him to immediate combat, Pelias promised to make way for him; but there was a family matter to attend to first. The unquiet spirit of his cousin Phrixus had visited Pelias in dreams, demanding that the golden fleece should be brought back from Colchis to Iolkos; Pelias was now too old to undertake the journey, but Jason was suitable in age and courage.

The story of the voyage of Jason and his chosen companions is familiar. Homer speaks of it only once, but it is probably one of the most ancient of the heroic sagas; it seems that many of the adventures ascribed by Homer to Odysseus and so located, presumably, in the Mediterranean came into being as part of the legend of Jason's expedition, and so were first imagined as happening in the Black Sea or its approaches. Most of us first hear the story told from the moment of Jason's first encounter with Pelias, and therefore see it only from the point of view of Jason. But if one knows the early history of the house of Aeolus, one may well side with the 'usurper' Pelias. If Pelias had sailed after the fleece, he as a son of Poseidon might well have faced Aeetes in combat, instead of winning the fleece through the love of a woman, escaping through a cowardly murder and finally betraying the person to whom he owed not only his triumph but his life.

But the ram who saved Phrixus is not the only ram we find identified with the leader of the Zodiac. Lucian in his treatise on astrology identified the latter with the golden lamb who figures in the story of Atreus, king of Argos and father of the famous Agamemnon, and of his disastrous quarrel with his brother Thyestes. Perhaps in both cases the golden colour of the fleece was thought appropriate to the faint glow of the stars that compose the constellation.

According to the best-known version of the story, Atreus' possession of the Argive throne was challenged by Thyestes. Called upon by the brothers to settle the dispute, Zeus sent to Atreus a golden lamb, a symbol of sovereignty, just as it is in a certain Persian folktale. But Atreus happened to be married to Aerope, a princess of that Cretan house whose female members were more than once involved in scandal (see p. 38). Thyestes made love to her and managed to persuade her to steal the lamb and place it in his hands. In the midst of the celebrations, just as Atreus was about to be proclaimed king, Thyestes produced the lamb and demanded that he should be enthroned in his brother's place.

Horrified at the treachery of Thyestes, Zeus produced a portent even more startling than the golden lamb. He caused the sun to change his course, turning day into night and night into day. So Atreus was recognised as king;

Aries

Aerope was drowned and Thyestes banished. But later Atreus lured his hated brother back to Argos with the promise of a reconciliation. He entertained him at a splendid banquet, at which a delicious dish of meat was served; only when Thyestes had eaten some and had expressed his appreciation was he told that he had been eating the flesh of his own children. Kicking over the table, Thyestes uttered a terrible curse upon his brother; then he departed into exile, and asked an oracle how he could obtain revenge. The answer was that he could do so only by begetting a son upon his own daughter. His surviving daughter, Pelopia, had been sent for safety's sake to Sicyon; he followed her there, and in disguise surprised her in a sacred grove near a temple where she had gone to sacrifice and there raped her. Her son by her father was Aegisthus, who later grew up to seduce the wife of Agamemnon and with her to plot his murder.

Some versions of this story make Zeus reverse the course of the sun in anger at the atrocious banquet offered to Thyestes, and this is indeed more shocking than Thyestes' treachery. But these appear to be secondary; the original tale seems to have been that the throne was to go to him who could produce the more marvellous portent, and that Atreus was able to overtrump the lamb, given to him but stolen by his brother, with the still more amazing portent of the sun's change of course. Lucian, who lived during the second century A.D., seems to be the only extant writer who identifies the heavenly ram with the lamb of the Thyestes legend rather than the familiar ram who carried Phrixus to Colchis.

Aries is a fiery sign, ruled by the planet Mars; his fire is the primal fire that creates and destroys. Aries types are juvenile, primitive, reckless, enthusiastic, easily angered; they have broad shoulders, walk fast and grip your hand firmly. Female Aries types are independent in regard to fashion; often they disdain the use of artificial aids to beauty.

II. Taurus

The Bull   April 21 to May 21

South of Perseus, north of Orion, near the feet of Auriga we find Taurus. The Babylonians do not seem to have thought the constellation like a bull; but the Greeks called it one, from early in the fifth century B.C. The stars known as the Hyades really do make up a figure resembling a bull's head, with the bright star Aldebaran as one of its eyes, although the head is decidedly three-cornered. How much of the bull can be seen in addition to the head is a disputed question. Artists usually present the front half of the bull only; he has sunk down upon one knee with lowered head as though to butt his adversary, pointing in the direction of the next Zodiacal sign, Gemini. Part of his body is made up by the famous cluster of the Pleiades, surrounding the third-magnitude star Alcyone; seven can be seen in a clear sky, and that is the canonical number, though others are visible even to the naked eye in good conditions. The five stars that form his head are the Hyades, one of the most beautiful constellations in the sky.

Three different bulls in mythology claim the honour of being identified with the celestial bull. One is the bull that carried Europa from her home in Tyre to Crete at the command of Zeus; one is the Cretan bull with which Pasiphae, wife of the great king Minos, so inopportunely fell in love; another, which indeed is no bull but a cow, is said to have been placed in the sky by Zeus in honour of his beloved Io.

Europa, daughter of the king of Tyre, Agenor, was playing by the seashore with her attendant maidens when they noticed a bull of most exceptional size and beauty. His colour was a golden brown, except for a white circle on his forehead; unlike most bulls he was quiet and gentle, and licked Europa's swanlike neck in most affectionate fashion. The bull kneeled down in front of the princess so invitingly that she could not help clambering upon his back. She invited some of her companions to join her there; but they hesitated, and in a moment the bull had risen to his feet and started out to sea. Not even the ram with the golden fleece was a better swimmer; and the journey was not uncomfortable, for the waves were calm and dolphins and other creatures of the sea gambolled around the bull and

36

the alarmed passenger clinging to his horns. At last the land disappeared from sight; night began to fall, and poor Europa could see nothing but the waves and the stars above them.

Europa soon guessed that her abductor was no real bull. She prayed to Poseidon, god of the sea, for his protection; but the bull now spoke to her, in reassuring tones. He told her that he was Zeus himself, and that he was taking her to Crete, where she would bear him famous sons. Her sons were Minos, the famous legendary king of Crete, Rhadamanthys who for his righteousness was made a judge in the world of the dead, and Sarpedon who was the bravest of the allies who fought on the side of Troy against the Greeks.

In most versions of Europa's story, the bull turns out to be Zeus himself, but that would not prevent him from placing a bull in the sky in memory of his exploit. That Zeus wooed Europa in the form of a bull is wholly consonant with Cretan myth, in which bulls played a most important part, as any visitor to Minos' palace of Knossos may see today. Minos married Pasiphae, a daughter of the Sun and sister of the Colchian king Aeetes and the enchantress Circe (see p. 31). One day a magnificent bull appeared out of the sea; it had been sent by Zeus as a sign that he recognised Minos as his son, and Minos should have sacrificed it to his father. But in his pride in the possession of so magnificent a beast, Minos kept the bull among his herds. There was an awful consequence, for Zeus in his anger caused Pasiphae to become infatuated with the splendid animal. Seeing no possible way of gratifying her passion, the queen began to pine away, very much as her daughter Phaedra was later to pine for love of her handsome stepson Hippolytus.

But at the court of Minos there was a man of infinite resource, capable, if any human being was capable, of finding a way for Pasiphae to satisfy her strange passion. This was the craftsman Daedalus, who had fled to Crete from his native Athens; jealous of a nephew who threatened to surpass him in his skill, he had made away with him and had to leave the country. He was the greatest craftsman living, able to make statues so perfectly lifelike that they could even move and speak. In the greatest secrecy the queen consulted Daedalus, and he promised he would do his best for her. He made a model of a cow of perfect beauty, calculated to deceive any bull; the cow was hollow, and when the moment came for use, the queen took her place inside it. In consequence she became pregnant, and the infant proved to be a monstrous mixture between man and bull, the Minotaur, or Bull of Minos.

Pasiphae tried hard to keep the birth a secret from her husband, but without success. The king's indignation knew no bounds; he threatened his wife with immediate execution. It happens that a papyrus found in Egypt in modern times preserves the speech Pasiphae made in her defence in the *Cretans*, the play Euripides wrote about the episode. 'If I were to deny the fact', the queen said, 'you would never believe me; it is clear enough. Now if I had prostituted my body in clandestine love to a man, you could have rightly said I was a whore. But as things are, it was a god who drove me mad; I am sorry, but it was not my fault. It makes no sense; what is it about the bull that could have stirred up my feelings with such a shameful passion? Did he look so splendid in his robes? Did his auburn hair and his eyes flash brilliantly? Was it his dark beard? It can hardly have been the symmetry of his form! This is the love for which I got into the skin and went on all fours; and this makes Minos angry! I could hardly wish to make *this* husband the father of children; why was I afflicted with this madness? It was *Minos'* evil genius who afflicted me with his curse; the one human being who bears all the guilt is *Minos*! It was he who broke the promise he had made to sacrifice the bull that came as a portent to the seagod. It was for *this* that Poseidon's vengeance came upon you, and it is on *me* that it descended! And then you cry aloud and call all the gods to witness, when the doer of the act that put me to shame is you yourself! I who gave birth to the creature have done no harm; I kept secret the godsent affliction of the curse. It is you who publish to all your wife's disgrace, handsome as it is and proper to display, as though you had no part in it, maddest of madmen! You are my ruin, because the crime is yours; you are the cause of my affliction! Well, if you wish to drown me, drown me! You are expert in bloody deeds and murder. Or if you lust to eat my flesh, then eat it, feed to your heart's content! I shall perish free and guiltless, for a crime for which *you* are guilty!'

Unfortunately we do not know how this play ended; but it looks as though a god appeared to protect Pasiphae and pacify her husband's wrath. To give the Minotaur a home, Minos caused Daedalus to construct the endlessly complicated maze known as the Labyrinth. Then another tragedy struck the great king; his only son Androgeos was murdered in Athens. Minos thought of a way of punishing the Athenians and pleasing his wife's monstrous son at the same time. Every year, the Athenians were forced to send seven men and seven maidens to Crete; there they were sent into the Labyrinth for the monster to devour. This continued until the great hero Theseus, the son of the Athenian king Aegeus, volunteered to go himself as one of the twice seven and with the indispensable aid of Minos' own daughter Ariadne managed to kill the Minotaur; but that story is familiar to all readers.

Early in this century the discovery of the great palace of Knossos by the English archaeologist Sir Arthur Evans threw much light on Cretan myths. The legend of the Labyrinth seems to have been inspired by the great palace itself, with its vast extent and labyrinthine complications. Bulls figure frequently in Minoan art; frescoes depict young men and woman leaping upon their backs. The bull was the sacred beast of the great god of Minoan Crete, identified by the later Greeks with Zeus. The god himself might be imagined in bull's shape, so that it was natural that Zeus should woo Europa as a bull and that Pasiphae should be the mother of the Bull of Minos.

After the discovery of Pasiphae's predicament, Minos was still confronted with the problem of how the bull which was responsible for it should be disposed of. The angry Poseidon had turned it savage, so that it now constituted a public menace. Luckily for the Cretans, this was the time when the great hero Heracles was obliged to perform twelve labours at the order of his cousin Eurystheus, king of Argos, and one of these labours was to subdue the Cretan Bull. Minos refused to furnish any help, but Heracles pursued the bull, caught it by a horn, and forced it to the ground. Some say that after he had brought it to Eurystheus it escaped again, and wandered from the Peloponnese into Attica. Here it did enormous damage, until the killer of the Minotaur, Theseus, dealt with it in the neighbourhood of Marathon.

The third candidate for identification with the bull in the sky is not a bull, but a cow, Io, daughter of Inachus, king of Argos in the very earliest times. Io was priestess in the great temple of Hera. She was visited by regularly recurring dreams, in which voices asked her why she chose to remain a virgin when she could become the bride of no less a god than Zeus. They urged her to go down to the marshy meadows of Lerna, near the coast, where her father's cattle used to graze, so that Zeus might be relieved of his desire. Io told her father of these dreams, and he sent envoys to the oracles of

Taurus

Apollo at Delphi and of Zeus at Dodona to enquire their meaning. At first the responses were obscure; then Inachus was ordered to turn his daughter out of doors, to wander through the wildest part of his dominions, and was warned that if he disobeyed his whole family would be exterminated by thunderbolts. Much against his will, Inachus complied.

As soon as Io had arrived in the remote territories of the Argolid, she underwent a startling transformation; Hera, jealous as ever of a rival, turned the unfortunate girl into a cow. To torment her she sent a relentless gadfly, who drove her towards Lerna and its watery meadows. There she was watched over by a faithful servant of Hera called Argos. Some say that he had extra eyes in the back of his head, but others say that his whole body was covered with them, and some of them were always open. Hera knew that Zeus was determined to rescue Io, and was taking no chances.

In his expeditions after mortal women Zeus often made use of the skill and cunning of his son and messenger Hermes, who was to him more than Leporello was to Don Giovanni. So now a handsome young shepherd introduced himself to Argos, who was glad of company in his lonely watch. The young shepherd was an incomparable story-teller; he told story after story, each more gripping than the last. But gradually the stories, without losing any of their fascination, became more and more calculated to send a listener to sleep. One by one, Argos' innumerable eyes closed in slumber. With infinite patience Hermes waited; as the last eye closed, he moved like lightning to take his chance. A sharp stone, the weapon that lay nearest to hand, smashed into the giant's face; and as he fell Hermes was upon him with his knife. All that Hera could do for her faithful servant was to preserve his memory by placing his numerous eyes in the tail of her favourite bird the peacock.

Now, it seemed, the coast was clear; but as Argos breathed his last the unhappy cow darted off at headlong speed, maddened by the savage biting of the gadfly. As she fled, Io seemed to see the ghost of Argos coming after her; 'not even in death' she exclaimed, 'does the earth cover him!' So she passed out of the Argolid, across the Isthmus of Corinth and into Attica; then she turned northward and raced through northern Greece; next she turned eastward and rushed along the coast of Thrace, finally crossing into Asia at the place the Greeks thought was named from 'the crossing of the cow', the Bosporus. Turning southwards, Io passed right through Asia Minor; then

41

she turned westwards, coming to a halt only when she had reached Egypt. Here at last her divine lover came to her rescue; by a mystic laying on of hands he restored her human shape and caused her to give birth to a son, Epaphus. Many generations later her descendant, Danaus, left Egypt with his daughters for Argos, the home of his ancestress, and his grandson occupied the Argive throne.

Like the myths about the Cretan bull, the myth of Io has a close link with religion. In the early versions of the story Io seems to have gone no further than Euboea, an island whose name signifies 'rich in cows'. But when the Greeks made their way to Egypt, they must have seen many statues of the cowheaded goddess Isis, and as usual tried to explain them in terms of their own religion. A woman who was partly cow—in some versions of the legend Io is only partially transformed—reminded them of Io, so Io's journey was prolonged as far as Egypt. This story fitted in well with the tradition that the royal house of Argos traced its ancestry from Egypt, just as the kings of Crete and Thebes traced theirs to Tyre.

It is not surprising that Zeus was thought to have honoured Io by placing her in the sky; he surely owed her handsome compensation for what she had gone through.

The five or, according to some, seven stars that form the bull's head are called the Hyades; some connect this with the Greek word for rain, but others take the word to mean 'piglets'. Several myths are connected with these stars, but above all they are identified with the daughters of Erechtheus, king of Athens in very early times.

A papyrus published only in 1967 contains parts of Euripides' play about Erechtheus that tells us of the legend about his daughters. When Athens was founded, Athene and Poseidon competed for the honour of being the new city's patron deity. On the Acropolis of Athens, near where the temple of Erechtheus now stands, the two divinities faced one another in the presence of the first king of Athens; each gave a demonstration of power meant to influence the king's choice. Poseidon struck the hard rock with his trident, and out of it sprang a superb white horse. Then Athena rapped the ground before her with her spear, and from it a beautiful olive tree sprouted into life. The Persians found this tree still growing when they occupied the Athenian Acropolis in 480 B.C.; they destroyed it, as they destroyed the temples. But when the Athenians reoccupied the city after their defeat, they found that the

Taurus

sacred olive had again put forth a shoot. The king chose Athena, wisely; but his choice was bound to infuriate Poseidon, and the new city had to face a severe crisis.

A son of Poseidon, the great warrior Eumolpus, had come from Thrace in the north and established his power in Eleusis, a few miles west of Athens. With a powerful army he marched against the Athenians, and their king Erechtheus knew that he must fight desperately for survival. He consulted the oracle at Delphi, and the response Apollo gave him was no less terrible than that which Agamemnon had received at Aulis (see p. 30). Athens could triumph only if a daughter of Erechtheus were sacrificed to appease Poseidon. The eldest offered herself, and the others chose voluntarily to share her fate.

The spirits of the dead princesses did not go to Hades; Athena carried them up to the ethereal fire above the sky. They became the object of an official cult of the Athenian state, and sacrifices were offered at their altar before an army marched out to war. They were called the Hyacinthides, and were often identified with the Hyades.

Part of the bull's body is made up by a still more famous group of stars, the Pleiades or Pleiads. Though their canonical number is seven, there are really more than forty; in May their rising marked the beginning of the harvest, and in November their setting the beginning of ploughing. Their name means 'doves', so that they are sometimes depicted in that shape; some equate them with the doves that carried ambrosia to feed the infant Zeus. They were the daughters of the Titan Atlas, brother of Prometheus, who for his part in the war waged by the Titans against Zeus was made to stand holding the heavens upon his shoulders. One of the seven shines faintly and is seldom visible; this is Electra, wife of Dardanus who founded Troy. After the destruction of the city founded by her husband, she withdrew her light from mortals.

Oddly the Bull counts as a feminine sign; its ruler among the planets is Venus. It is a fixed sign, an earthy sign; Taurus types are slow, strong, persistent. One understands their nature best if one thinks of Taurus as an ox.

III. Gemini

The Twins   May 22 to June 21

Beneath the head of the Lesser Bear are the Twins, one of the most splendid of the northern constellations; the Milky Way passes through it. It takes its name from its two brightest stars, one of the first and one of the second magnitude. Some authorities identified them with Heracles and Apollo; but Heracles and Apollo, although half-brothers, were not twins. They have been identified with two famous pairs of twins; sometimes with Zethus and Amphion, but more often with Castor and Polydeuces, or Pollux. Pollux is by far the brighter star, and rightly, for unlike his brother he was immortal by nature. Zethus and Amphion were sons of Zeus by Antiope, daughter of the Boeotian hero Nycteus; to get his way with her, Zeus took the form of a satyr, one of the lascivious creatures with horse's tail and legs (the goat-legged satyr comes later) who followed in the train of Dionysus. When her father learned that she was pregnant, Antiope fled from her home in Boeotia to Epopeus, king of Sicyon, a place in the Peloponnese not far from Corinth. This so distressed Nycteus that he committed suicide, leaving the task of punishing his daughter to his brother Lycus, who had now usurped the Theban throne. In the resulting war Epopeus was killed and Antiope was taken prisoner. In her captivity she gave birth to twin sons, whom she was forced to expose; they were found and brought up by a herdsman who was herding cattle. The resemblance to the myth of Tyro is very striking (see p. 32).

But Zethus and Amphion were more unlike in character than the sons of Tyro. Zethus was strong and energetic, and applied himself successfully to their foster-father's work of breeding cattle; but Amphion received the gift of a lyre from the god Hermes, and played upon it with a master's skill. Zethus could not understand his brother's addiction to what seemed to him a womanish pursuit, and bitterly reproached him with its uselessness. But Amphion energetically defended the value of art and of the intellectual life: and Euripides in his play *Antiope* made their debate a classic instance of the clash between the two outlooks which they represented.

For long years Antiope dragged out a miserable life, persecuted by Lycus

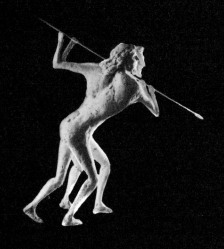

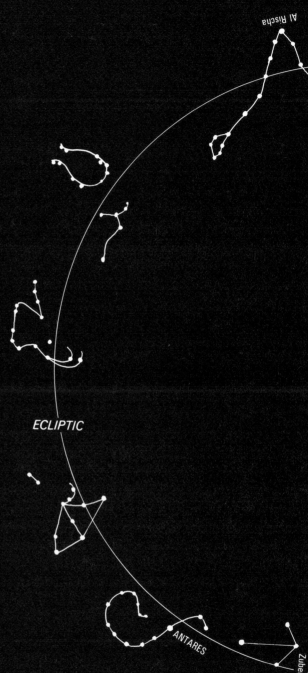

Al Rischa

ECLIPTIC

ANTARES

Zubenelgenubi

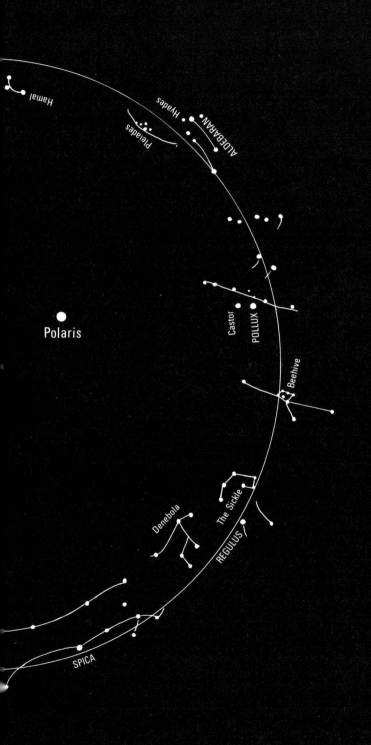

Hamal

Pleiades

Hyades

ALDEBARAN

Polaris

Castor

POLLUX

Beehive

Denebola

The Sickle

REGULUS

SPICA

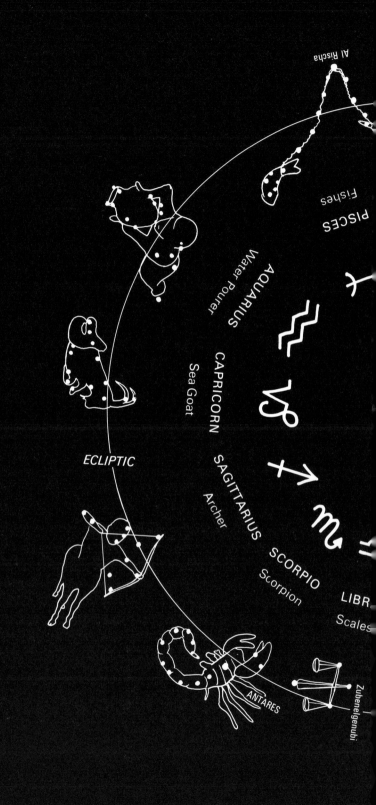

and his cruel wife Dirce. At last her existence became so intolerable that she fled from their palace and came to the humble dwelling of some herdsmen to seek refuge. Here she found her two sons, and asked them for help; neither she nor they were aware of the other's identity. At first Zethus was unwilling to help, taking his mother for a runaway slave, but Amphion was more understanding. Dirce now arrived in the neighbourhood, having travelled to the mountains to celebrate a Bacchic festival, and the unfortunate Antiope again fell into her hands. But now the brothers, talking with the old herdsman who had brought them up, found out their real identity and their mother's. They ambushed Dirce's party, routed her escort, and rescued Antiope. A famous group of statuary in Naples depicts the terrible revenge they took on Dirce; they tied her to a wild bull and let it loose to drag her over the mountains till she perished. Setting out in search of her, Lycus too fell into the hands of Zethus and Amphion; some say that he was killed, but in Euripides' famous play he was saved by the intervention of the god Hermes. But the god ordered Lycus to give up the Theban kingship to the brothers, who now built the city's celebrated walls. Zethus used his vast strength to perform prodigies of labour; but his contribution was no greater than that of Amphion, who by his music so charmed stones and trees that they came into position of their own accord.

Amphion married Niobe, daughter of the great Phrygian ruler Tantalus, and she gave birth to seven sons and seven daughters, all of surpassing beauty. But Niobe was so unwise as to remark to Leto, mother by Zeus of Artemis and Apollo, that she herself had seven sons and seven daughters, while Leto had only one child of each sex. The gods did not forgive such insolence. Apollo shot down Niobe's sons while they were hunting on Mount Cithaeron, Artemis her daughters at home in the palace. Aeschylus and Sophocles both wrote plays about this subject; both are lost, but modern papyrus discoveries have thrown light on each. The play of Aeschylus begins two days after the death of the children; ever since Niobe has sat by their tomb in silent lamentation. In the play by Sophocles Apollo calls out to his sister as she is shooting down the daughters, 'Do you see the frightened one inside?,' he says, 'the one cowering in the storeroom, by the great jars? Quick, shoot her before she escapes out of sight!' These remorseless words recall the calm, expressionless face of the Apollo who on the east pediment of the temple of Zeus at Olympia towers over the battle between the Lapiths

Gemini

and the Centaurs who are trying to carry off their women (see p. 82). One daughter, Chloris, did survive the massacre; she married Neleus and gave birth to Nestor (see p. 33).

The twins in the sky are more often associated with a pair of twins more famous than Zethus and Amphion. These are the sons of Leda, wife of Tyndareus, king of Sparta. To win her favours Zeus changed himself into a swan and Hermes, his usual assistant in such matters, into an eagle. When Leda was bathing in the river Eurotas, near Sparta, the eagle pursued the swan, who took refuge in the arms of the Spartan queen. In consequence, she laid two eggs of giant size. From one emerged a son, Castor, and a daughter, Clytemnestra, both the offspring of Leda's mortal husband, Tyndareus; from the other came a son, Polydeuces (in Latin Pollux) and a daughter, the incomparable Helen, both the offspring of Zeus.

That, at least, is the version usually current in classical times. But originally both Castor and Pollux must have been thought of as sons of Zeus; they are often called the Dioscuri, which means precisely that. They were great horsemen and great charioteers; some say that they invented chariots. In historical times they counted not as gods but as heroes; but at Sparta their cult, like that of their sister Helen, was of great importance, and originally they were gods, whose worship goes back to the earliest age of Indo-European religion. From the Vedas we learn that the early Indians knew them under the name of the Asvins; in Lithuania, which remained pagan till the thirteenth century and preserved many ancient myths, we find a similar pair of divine horsemen. Zethus and Amphion are simply the Boeotian version of the same couple. Sailors on the sea prayed to the Dioscuri, and they gave them courage by perching on the masts of ships caught in a storm in the form of the phenomenon known as St. Elmo's Fire.

Cities and individuals who honoured the Dioscuri found them reliable protectors. The great poet Simonides of Ceos once wrote a poem of praise commissioned by a Thessalian prince. This patron complained that the poem said more in praise of the Dioscuri than in praise of him; in doing so he showed himself ignorant as well as irreverent, for it was customary for poems written to praise men to praise the gods also, and to remind the former that they could achieve nothing without the favour of the latter. When Simonides demanded the customary fee, the prince refused to pay, suggesting that he should ask the Dioscuri to reward him. That evening when the prince and his friends and visitors were feasting in his banquet-hall, Simonides was called from the table by a servant, who told him that two young men were at the door and wished to speak with him. The moment the poet had left the hall, its roof fell in and everyone there perished; the Dioscuri had paid Simonides for his poem by making sure that he escaped.

The Dioscuri would ride to battle to fight on the side of cities that had honoured them, and such cities were always victorious. They fought on the side of Sparta against Athens when Lysander won his great victory at Aegospotami; it was owing to their help that ten thousand Locrians vanquished ten times as many Crotoniates at the battle of the Sagra. Their cult was established at Rome from early times, and all readers of Macaulay's *Lays of Ancient Rome* remember how they fought for Rome in the great battle of Lake Regillus against the Etruscan army that was trying to restore the rule of the tyrannical king Tarquin.

When Jason summoned the greatest heroes of Greece to help him recover the golden fleece from Colchis (see p. 34), the Dioscuri joined him. On the way to the kingdom of Aeetes the ship stopped in the territory of the Bebryces, in the north of Asia Minor. This people was ruled by a brutal tyrant, Amycus, who forced strangers to box with him, using the terrible boxing-gloves of raw hide favoured by the ancients, and who up to that time had killed everyone who had stood up to him. When the Argonauts landed, Castor and Pollux strayed away from their companions, and by a fountain encountered this terrifying brute, with cauliflower ears, bulging chest and swelling muscles. Boastfully Amycus challenged the best boxer on the ship to fight him, and Pollux took up the challenge. As the two faced up to each other the young hero seemed to be no match for the formidable bruiser; but in speed and skill he was easily superior, and he did not lack strength. Neatly sidestepping Amycus' blind rush, Pollux caught him on the chin with an uppercut that drove him almost berserk. The wilder his blows became, the more easily did his opponent dodge them, repeatedly darting his fists to the monster's face. At last Amycus came to a standstill, spitting blood; and now Pollux landed a tremendous punch above his nose, skinning his forehead to the bone and knocking him flat upon his back. Amycus rose and came again at his opponent, but his blows kept missing, while those of Pollux kept finding their mark. At last Amycus grasped his opponent's left hand with his own and swung at him with his right; but Pollux dodged the blow and struck at his enemy's left temple, following up with a left to the mouth that rattled Amycus' teeth. Down went Amycus and held up both hands in token of surrender. Some say that he actually perished in the fight; but our best authority, the Hellenistic poet Theocritus, says that the victor was content to make him swear a great oath that he would never again molest a stranger.

Many poets number the Dioscuri among the heroes who answered the call of the Aetolian prince Meleager for volunteers to hunt the gigantic wild boar which Artemis had sent to ravage the lands of his father Oeneus. They are depicted in the most famous representation of the hunt, that on the François Vase, in Florence, painted in about 570 B.C. It is a great mixing-bowl nearly 27 inches high and decorated all over with rows of small figures. In front, on the upper zone of the neck, we see the hunting of a boar. First blood has been drawn by the only woman in the party, the virgin huntress Atalanta; three arrows have hit the boar, but three hounds and the axe-wielding hero Ancaeus are lying dead. The death-stroke will be delivered by Meleager, who with Peleus, father of Achilles, in support strikes at the boar's open jaws; behind the boar, the two Dioscuri grasping the same great spear are about to plunge it into the boar's back. The outline of the stars corresponds with the twins' position on the vase (and in the illustration).

Helen, the sister of the Dioscuri, was so beautiful that not even the knowledge that she had brothers as formidable as they were could prevent men from trying to abduct her. The great Athenian hero Theseus once made an unholy pact with his friend Pirithous, king of the Lapiths in Thessaly (see p. 82). Each was to help the other to carry off a daughter of Zeus to be his bride; Theseus was to kidnap Helen, then only twelve years old, and then the pair were to descend to Hades with the even more hazardous intention of carrying off Persephone, wife of its ruler, Hades or Pluto. Waiting till the Dioscuri were away from home, the pair lay in wait for Helen as she danced at the temple of Artemis not far from Sparta. Safely back in Attica, they gave Helen for safe-keeping to Aphidnus, whose town of Aphidna was in north-east Attica, near Rhamnus and Marathon. There Helen was placed under the care of Theseus' mother Aethra while the two friends left for Epirus in the north of Greece, one of the places where one might descend to the underworld.

They were away longer than they had planned, for their expedition was a disastrous failure. Their plan was to give the appearance of paying a friendly visit to Hades, who gave them a polite reception. But the seat on which he seated them was the Seat of Forgetfulness, from which it was impossible, once you had sat down, to rise. Some say that Pirithous stayed there for ever. Theseus was luckier, for the next visitor from the upper world happened to be his friend Heracles. With a mighty wrench Heracles managed to drag Theseus free, with damage to his anatomy which later supplied material for jokes about certain peculiarities attributed to his people, the Athenians. Theseus consoled himself with the thought that when he returned the beautiful Helen would be awaiting him; but when he arrived home, she was there no longer.

Helen's brothers had returned, and had set out for Athens, threatening war if their sister were not handed over. Those in charge at Athens were alarmed, but were genuinely ignorant of her whereabouts, which had been kept a closely guarded secret. Somehow the secret became known to the hero Decelus, and he betrayed it to the invaders. During the Peloponnesian War in the late fifth century B.C., the invading Spartan armies were careful to avoid damaging his town of Deceleia, west of Aphidna; finally on the advice of the renegade Athenian general Alcibiades they made it their main base in Attica. A later story says that the secret was betrayed by the hero Academus; it was in a gymnasium in his precinct outside Athens that Plato taught, thus causing the word 'academy' to acquire its present meaning. The Dioscuri laid siege to Aphidna and soon took it. Another local hero, Titacus, betrayed it; Theseus, who unified Attica under Athens, was not very popular with local heroes. Helen was recovered, and Aethra was brought to Sparta as a prisoner. Later, when Helen had grown up and married Menelaus, Aethra was still one of her attendants when Paris came and persuaded her to run away with him to Troy; and it was only after Troy had fallen that the aged lady was recovered by her grandsons, fighting on the Greek side. Helen is said to have returned to Sparta none the worse for her experience in Attica. Owing to her tender years Theseus respected her virginity; but the comic poets suggested that he permitted himself certain pleasures which might be indulged in without breach of his resolution, and this belief gave rise to more stock jokes about Athenian habits.

Not everyone, however, accepted Theseus' denial. The usual legend makes Iphigenia the daughter of Agamemnon by his wife Clytemnestra; but some poets claim that she was really a love-child of Clytemnestra's sister

Gemini

Helen by Theseus, and was given to Clytemnestra to bring up as her own.

By the time their sister married Menelaus, the Dioscuri were no longer in the land of the living. They had long been rivals of their cousins Idas and Lynceus, and in them they had enemies not unworthy of their steel. Lynceus had the sharpest eyesight of any mortal man; not only could he see a long way, but he could see through objects. Idas was a great warrior, ready to confront even a god. He carried off Marpessa, the daughter of the river god Evenus; driving away with her in his chariot, he found the way barred by Apollo, who ordered him to hand her over. As they prepared to fight, a thunderbolt hurtled into the ground between them; Zeus had decided to let Marpessa choose between them. Marpessa chose the human lover, who might not desert her after one encounter, and Apollo had to let her go. Idas sailed after the golden fleece, and was always the advocate of violent resistance; the subtle and tactful Jason had difficulty in persuading him not to commit rash actions that might have led to a disaster.

Idas and Lynceus quarrelled with their cousins, either over a pair of female cousins, the Leucippides (Rubens in his great painting in Munich shows how they were carried off) or simply over cattle. High among the peaks of Taygetus, the great mountain range that looms over Sparta and the valley of the Eurotas, the Dioscuri were hiding inside a hollow oaktree. But the keen eyesight of Lynceus could still find them out; he signalled to his brother, and running silently and swiftly they caught up their opponents. In a moment Idas had stabbed Castor with his brazen spear. 'At once,' says the poet Pindar, 'Polydeuces started in pursuit; and near their father's tomb they took their stand against him. From it they wrenched an ornament of Hades, a polished stone, and smashed it into Polydeuces' chest. But they failed to crush him or to drive him back; and darting swiftly at them with his javelin he drove the bronze into the ribs of Lynceus. Then Zeus hurled upon Idas his fire-bearing sooty thunderbolt, and together they were burned; to fight against those whose power is greater is too much for men. But quickly back to his brother went the son of Tyndareus, and he found him not yet dead, but breathing in great gasps. Shedding hot tears and groaning, he cried out aloud, 'Father, son of Kronos, what can save me from my sorrow? Grant to me too death, my lord! A man's honour is lost when he loses those who love him, and few mortals can be trusted to take their share of labour in time of trouble'. So he spoke, and Zeus came to him and said these words, 'You are my son; but this man comes from the mortal seed the hero sowed when he came to your mother. Come now, I give you the choice! If you wish to escape death and hateful old age, and to live on Olympus with me and with Athanaia and with Ares of the black spear, you have a right to this. But if you fight for your brother and you have a mind to share equally in all things, you may spend half your time beneath the earth and half in the golden halls of heaven!' Hearing these words, Polydeuces did not debate the matter in his mind, but opened the eye of Castor of the brazen helmet, and made his voice sound again.'

Gemini is a mutable and airy sign, ruled by Mercury. Gemini types enjoy argument; they are clever, but a little cold. Among them we find men of genius, like Dante; we also find madmen, crooks, and very selfish people.

IV. Cancer

The Crab   June 22 to July 22

The furthest point north which the sun reaches is in the sign of Cancer, which lies between Gemini and Leo. Its brightest stars are only of the fourth magnitude; its most interesting feature is the cluster Praesepe (the Latin word for Manger), sometimes called the beehive. Two Asses also form part of the Crab. For the Egyptians this constellation was a beetle; the Greeks seem to have been the first to call it a crab. The sun reaching the solstice seems to hover and move away after it has reached its zenith; perhaps that suggested the crab's sideways motion.

One of the most formidable of the twelve labours imposed on Heracles by his cousin Eurystheus (see p. 40) was that of dealing with the Hydra, a monstrous watersnake which emerged daily from the marsh of Lerna near Argos to harry the fertile territory of the Argolid. Opinions differ about the number of its heads; some say it had as many as a hundred, but a good authority says that there were nine, one of which is immortal. Heracles set out from Lerna in a chariot driven by his nephew Iolaus, a great hero in his own right and his uncle's usual companion on his expeditions. The Hydra's den was on a hill, near the springs of the famous fountain called after Amymone, one of the fifty daughters of Danaus. For a long time it lay low, so that Heracles wondered whether it was at home; then he shot arrows with objects on fire tied to their ends into the cave, and that brought the Hydra out. Heracles got a firm grip of the Hydra, which coiled itself about one of his legs. Then he brought his mighty club into action, smashing a head with every blow; but no sooner was one destroyed than two more grew from the same root. Meanwhile the Hydra was joined by a new ally. All other creatures favoured Heracles; but out of the marsh came an immense crab, who with his pincers snapped at Heracles' feet. With one leg already in the Hydra's grip, this was as dangerous as it was painful. But the crab could not hold up Heracles for long. The Hydra left him no leisure to strike it with his club; but one foot was still free, and finally he stamped upon the crab's tough shell and crushed it so that it lay helpless. The battle with the Hydra might have lasted much longer; but Athene often helped the hero with her counsel,

59

and it was her suggestion that helped him to final victory. 'Send Iolaus,' she told him; 'into the wood; he must set a branch on fire, and every time you crush or lop off a head, he must hold it against the wound'. Iolaus obeyed, and now the new heads no longer sprouted, so that before long only the immortal head was left. Heracles drew his sword and swept it off, and at last the great snake collapsed in death. Heracles buried the immortal head on the road that leads from Lerna to Elaeus; over it he put a mighty rock, too heavy for any other man to lift. Then he dipped his arrows in the hydra's poisoned blood, making them fatal to anyone their points might touch. The poisoned arrows were to serve him well in countless battles; but in the end they were to prove fatal not only to Heracles' friend the Centaur Chiron, but to Heracles himself (see pp. 82f.).

Hera was always loyal to her faithful servants, and like Argos (see p. 41) the brave crab was not forgotten by his mistress. Hera promoted him to the sky, and one of the Tropics bears his name.

The two Asses are connected by more than one story with the god Dionysus. When Dionysus was born, Hera refused to accept him as a god (see p. 29), and persecuted him in every possible way. Only after a whole series of adventures did she withdraw her opposition, so that the new deity was able to take up his proper position on Olympus. His chance came with the disappearance of the lame craftsman god Hephaestus, son of Hera and Zeus. Hera was disgusted with this son because he was a cripple, as smiths often are in Greece today; she did not yet understand that he made up for his ugliness by his extraordinary powers. Hera threw him out of heaven; though it is only fair to mention that some say that it was Zeus who threw him out for having protected Hera against the not unreasonable anger of Zeus himself. The god fell to earth on the island of Lemnos, a place closely associated with his worship; later Thetis and the other sea-nymphs took good care of him. He returned to Olympus, pretended to forgive his mother, and in token of reconciliation made her a present of a wonderful throne which he had made. Hera proudly took her seat upon it; but the moment she had sat down, she found it impossible to rise. Only Hephaestus had the power to free her, and he was nowhere to be found. It was imperative for the gods to fetch Hephaestus back to release his mother; and now Dionysus saw his chance. Accompanied by his old tutor, the perpetually drunken Silenus, and the other satyrs, Dionysus set out after Hephaestus. Other gods

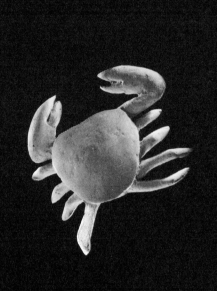

laughed at the notion that Dionysus might succeed. The war-god Ares was confident that he could conquer Hephaestus and bring him back in chains; but he knew nothing about artillery. Hephaestus invented a form of it, and Ares was completely routed.

Dionysus had a better weapon. When he had found Hephaestus, he pointed out that they were half-brothers, and argued that since each had a grudge against the other gods they should be friends. He was able to offer the most delicious wine, which at his command flowed from trees and rivers. Making Hephaestus royally drunk, he captured him without a struggle; vase paintings show Dionysus and the satyrs bringing back Hephaestus in triumph to Olympus, the two gods mounted sometimes on mules, but oftener on asses. One account of the Asses in the sky is that they were those ridden by the two gods. When the gods fought their famous battle against the Giants at Pallene, in Chalcidice in the north of Greece, Dionysus and Hephaestus rode into battle on their asses, and the braying of the creatures helped to spread panic among the enemy.

A less familiar story is that Hera for a time contrived to send Dionysus mad. He knew that he could find a cure for his madness if he could contrive to reach the ancient oracle of Zeus at Dodona, in Epirus in the north of Greece, where in early times the answers seem to have been transmitted by the whispering branches of the sacred oaktrees. But the way to Dodona was barred by a great swamp, and Dionysus wondered how he was to get across it. Suddenly he saw approaching a herd of asses; he mounted on the back of one, and somehow the creature got him across the swamp without even getting his feet wet. Dionysus wished to reward his benefactor generously, and changed the somewhat unmusical voice with which nature had endowed him into human speech. But this gift nearly proved fatal for the poor ass. One day he encountered Priapus, a son of Dionysus by Aphrodite, a god whose worship spread from Lampsacus in Asia Minor, and who was noted for the enormous size of his private parts. The two quarrelled violently as to which was more richly endowed in this respect; judges were appointed, suitable conditions obtained, and a competition was held. Naturally the god was proclaimed the winner, and naturally he wished to take a terrible revenge upon his challenger, just as Apollo did upon the satyr Marsyas and the Muses upon the singer Thamyras. Priapus was about to kill the poor ass when Dionysus arrived to rescue his old benefactor. Another ass was sacrificed in his place, and to commemorate the incident both asses were placed among the stars, and given a manger so that they could keep off the pangs of hunger.

Cancer stands for the primal water, as Aries for the primal fire; its ruler is the Moon. It is feminine, vegetative, maternal, and stands for conception and fertility. Cancer types are sensitive and understanding; but if male they may display some feminine characteristics.

V. Leo

The Lion · July 23 to August 23

The stars of the Great Bear point directly to the splendid cluster of Leo, conspicuous in the southern sky on summer evenings. It is natural to associate lions with hot weather; and though in some Babylonian texts the constellation is called a dog, both Egyptians and Babylonians took it to be a lion from an early time. The lion looks westwards towards the crab, his head and tail projecting north of the Ecliptic. Regulus is his brightest star; that name means 'little king'. and has often been associated with royalty.

The Greeks usually identify the lion with the most formidable lion in their mythology, the lion that infested the Argolid from his lair at Nemea, south of Corinth and north of Argos, where afterwards the famous Nemean Games were held. This lion started its career, strangely enough, in the moon; it was conveyed to earth by Hera, who wished her enemy Heracles to have another dangerous adversary to cope with. It soon reduced the area around Nemea to a desert, since the peasants dared not venture out to feed their animals or sow their crops. When Hera's plotting obliged Heracles to perform twelve labours at the order of his cowardly cousin Eurystheus, the first task assigned him was to kill the Nemean Lion without weapons, and to display its hide before the king.

Heracles set out on foot for Cleonae, east of Nemea; the way was long, the sun was hot, and he was tired and hungry when he got there. Few people were about, but finally he received hospitality from an old peasant called Molorchus, who generously welcomed him to his humble home. Since his only son had been killed by the lion, he was eager to assist the hero; and he prepared to sacrifice the single ram that made up all his livestock in order to give him proper nourishment. Heracles with difficulty persuaded Molorchus to hold his hand. 'If I kill the lion,' he said, 'then you may sacrifice the ram to me as a god; if it kills me, you may sacrifice it to me as a hero.' Then he asked the old man to direct him to the lion's lair.

When Heracles got to Nemea, he set out to track down the lion. Once he was within range, he shot an arrow from his bow. The arrow struck the lion, but glanced off its tough hide; Hera had made the beast invulnerable.

64

Heaving up his great club, Heracles made after the beast, who turned tail and took refuge in his lair. This was in a cave with two mouths, so Heracles fetched stones to block up one of the two exits; then he entered the cave to track down the lion. In the darkness the two came face to face. Grasping the lion by the throat, Heracles exerted his whole mighty strength till he had choked the life from its body; then he laid it on his shoulders and set off for the hut where Molorchus lived.

Heracles had told Molorchus that if he was not back within a month he must presume him dead; and most of the month had now passed. He was tired, and it was very hot; so it was easy for Hera, who grudged him the honour of being sacrificed to as a god, to cause him to fall asleep. On the very last day of the month Heracles arrived, to find that Molorchus had sacrificed the ram to him in the way proper for a hero. This was a disappointment, for in a sacrifice to a hero he would get nothing to eat; but he managed to get there before all of his portion had been burned. In some places Heracles was sacrificed to as a god, in others as a hero, and in others as both at once; this story must have been invented to explain why Nemea, like Sicyon not far away, belonged in this category of places. It was natural to assume that so great a hero had a hearty appetite, and the comic poets told many stories of Heracles' greed; legends like this show how the idea originated.

Molorchus was rewarded by the hero with a present of a fine new mule. Heracles flayed the lion, and for ever afterwards used its hide as garment, shield or sleeping-bag; it is one of the attributes that make him easy to recognise in works of art.

A cluster of stars near the lion's tail acquired its name, the Lock of Berenice, through an incident of the year 246 B.C. The young king Ptolemy III, called Ptolemy Euergetes (The Benefactor), had not long occupied the throne of Egypt. In dramatic circumstances he had married his cousin Berenice, heiress to the neighbouring Greek kingdom of Cyrene. The fathers of the two had agreed on their betrothal; but Berenice's father had died, and her mother Apama had plotted to marry her to her own lover, Demetrius the Fair, so as to retain control of the kingdom for herself. With the courage and intelligence that marked so many of the women of her extraordinary family—Cleopatra VII, Antony's Cleopatra, was to be the last of them—the young princess at the head of her supporters carried through a *coup d'état*. Apama was overthrown, Demetrius was killed, and Berenice married her

Leo

cousin, not long before he succeeded to the throne of Egypt.

Almost immediately another danger threatened the royal couple. A sister of Ptolemy, another Berenice, had been married to Antiochus II of Syria as his second wife. When Antiochus died, Berenice was at once ejected by her husband's divorced first wife, Laodice, and the new king of Egypt had to leave his bride and march with an army to relieve his sister. Berenice vowed that if he returned safely she would dedicate a lock of her hair to all the gods and place it in a temple of Aphrodite where that goddess was identified with her husband's deceased step-mother Arsinoe.

Ptolemy arrived in Syria to find that his sister had already been murdered. But though he could not save her he was able to avenge her; and his forces soon overran the country. So Berenice fulfilled her vow; but almost at once the lock vanished from the temple. Its disappearance was turned to good account by the court astronomer, Conon, who reported that he had seen a new constellation in the sky, in which he had recognised the queen's hair. The discovery supplied the great poet Callimachus, who stood high in the favour of the royal house and as a Cyrenaean had a special link with Berenice, with the occasion for one of the greatest of all court poems. In a manner at once respectful and familiar, Callimachus put his poem into the mouth of the lock itself. It described how Zephyrus, the West Wind, had carried it from the temple to the sky, and how, greatly as it valued the honour done to it, it regretted the loss of its place among the queen's tresses.

Sometime after its original publication, this poem was placed at the end of the fourth and last book of the Aitia, a long poem in elegiac couplets in which Callimachus explained the origin of many cults and customs. Unlike the poet's Hymns and Epigrams, the Aitia failed to be handed down by the Byzantine scribes to modern times; until lately, we possessed only the few fragments that ancient writers happened to have quoted. But Catullus, the great Roman poet contemporary with Julius Caesar, made a magnificent translation of the *Lock of Berenice*. Then during the present century papyri found in Egypt made us acquainted with not much less than half of the original poem of Callimachus.

Leo is a fixed and fiery sign; his fire resembles molten gold. Leo types are large, fair and handsome, often haughty and ambitious; among them are Louis XIV, Napoleon and Bismarck, as well as many Presidents of the United States.

67

VI. Virgo

The Maiden   August 24 to September 23

Continuing through Arcturus the sweep from the tail of the Great Bear, one finds the bright star Spica, the ear of corn in the hand of the Maiden, who stands in the words of Aratus 'beneath both feet of Boötes'. She stands in the attitude of an archaic Greek statue, one arm down at the side, the other forward. Above the Maiden's shoulders is another bright star, Vindemiatrix, the Vintager. How early the constellation was identified as a Maiden remains obscure.

Aratus identifies the Maiden with the Greek goddess of Justice, Dike. Long before his time the eighth-century poet Hesiod had told how Dike was the daughter of Zeus, and how when men did violence against her she took her seat beside her father and denounced their wickedness, so that he would punish them. In the same poem, the *Works and Days*, (see p. 12) Hesiod told how four earlier races of mankind had perished, and how the fifth race, to which we belong, would finally so anger Zeus by its wickedness that he would destroy it also.

When that race reaches the peak of its evil-doing, Hesiod writes, 'there will depart from broad earth to Olympus, veiling their lovely faces beneath their white robes, leaving men and joining the immortals, the goddesses Aidos and Nemesis (= Respect and Just Apportionment); and grievous pain will be left for men, and they will have no defence against their troubles.'

This passage of Hesiod inspired Aratus in what he says of Dike. There is a story, he writes, that once the goddess lived on earth. 'She would meet men face to face', (he continues (*Phaenomena* 102f.), 'and did not reject the men or the women of ancient times, but would sit in their company, immortal as she was. They called her Dike, and she would gather together the elders in a market place or in a wide road and would chant to them just laws, urging them to obedience. In those days they knew nothing of hateful strife, nor of censorious disputation, nor of abuse.

'They lived free of all this; and the cruel sea was far away, and ships did not bring their means of living from distant parts, but all things were furnished to them by cattle and ploughs and by the queen of the people, Dike herself,

68

giver of Justice. This lasted so long as the earth maintained the golden race; but with the silver race she consorted rarely and less readily, for she missed the ways of the people of the former time. But none the less this still went on under the silver race; in the evenings she would come alone from the echoing mountains, though she no longer addressed anyone with kindly words, but when she had filled the great hills with men, she would threaten them, reproaching them for their wickedness, and said she would no longer appear to them when they called upon her. "What a race your golden fathers have left behind them! – a race worse than theirs, and your children shall be worse still. Men shall have wars, and enmity, and pain shall follow evil-doing". With these words she made for the mountains, and she left all the people still gazing after her. But when they too were dead, and others had been born, a race of bronze more destructive than earlier men, who first forged cruel swords that did murder on the roads, and first ate the oxen that drew their ploughs, then Dike conceived a hatred for the race of those men, and flew up to heaven; and she made her home in that place where by night she still appears to mortals, as the Virgin near the conspicuous Boötes.'

Hesiod's Dike is a punisher of crime; that of Aratus is more like a goddess of righteousness. There is nothing specifically Stoic in what he says about her; yet it is typical of the moral earnestness of this great Stoic poet, whose patron was the Stoic king of Macedonia, the conscientious Antigonus Gonatas.

Another famous poet of the same century offered quite a different identification of the celestial Maiden. The great geographer and mathematician, Eratosthenes of Cyrene, at one time royal librarian at Alexandria, was also a distinguished poet. In his most famous poem, called *Erigone*, he told how Dionysus first brought the gift of wine to mortals. He came first to the village of Icaria, in Attica, where he was generously entertained by its eponym, the peasant Icarius. Icarius told his daughter Erigone to milk the goat so as to obtain milk to give their guest; but the milk changed to wine, grapes grew from the floor, and a great mixing-bowl made its appearance. Icarius and his family were delighted with the new experience; and the god taught them how to grow vines and how to make wine out of their grapes.

When Icarius had a large quantity of wine available, he happened to catch his goat nibbling a vine. In a rage he killed the beast, and to help his family eat up the flesh asked in some neighbours, who were no less pleased with the

Virgo

new drink. After that Icarius travelled round Attica in a cart, bringing wine to village after village. But in one of these villages the inhabitants drank too much, and soon many were stretched out on the ground, heavily asleep. Their friends imagined that Icarius must have poisoned them. They fell upon him and battered him with spades and axes, finally finishing him off with a great stone. They loaded the body and the dead man's mixing-bowl onto his cart and threw it into a pond. When the friends they had supposed dead woke up and told them they had never slept better, the murderers were horrified, and sailed off to the neighbouring island of Ceos to live there instead.

When Icarius did not return, his daughter Erigone became anxious, and finally her father appeared to her in a dream and told what had happened. He begged her to find his body and to give it burial; but for a long time she searched for it in vain. Then she came upon his faithful dog Maira, who took a fold of her garment in her mouth and guided her to the pond into which the murderers had pushed the cart. Erigone put a curse upon them, adding that if the Athenians should fail to punish them their daughters should perish as she was about to perish. The she hanged herself from a tree; and Maira, after guiding some passers-by to the body, starved herself to death.

Erigone's curse was fulfilled; an epidemic of suicides broke out among the Athenian girls, and they hanged themselves in large numbers, as within living memory such an epidemic broke out among the girls of Hungary through the spell cast by a sad and haunting song. The citizens consulted the Delphic oracle, and were ordered to appease Erigone by honouring her with a festival. Herdsmen sang songs in Erigone's praise, and dolls and masks were hung in trees, so that they swung as Erigone had swung. Living girls also constructed swings and swung happily to and fro. This was the origin of the Athenian festival called Aiora, after the word for 'swing', which is illustrated by many delightful paintings on Athenian vases.

The parching heat of the Dog-Star had a devastating effect on the island of Ceos, where the murderers of Icarius had taken refuge; that star was none other than the faithful dog Maira, placed in the stars as a reward for her fidelity. Icarius himself is the Waggoner, Boötes; north-east of him is his Waggon, and his Oxen, and south-east of him his Mixing-Bowl. Between him and the Mixing-Bowl (Crater) is the Maiden, who according to Eratosthenes is identical with Erigone.

Luckily for the men of Ceos their king was Aristaeus, son of Apollo, who was able to ask his father for help and advice. Apollo ordered him to find the murderers of Icarius and punish them; after that, they were to sacrifice to Icarius and to offer special prayers to Zeus to send from the north a healing wind. That was the origin of the trade-winds, which start to blow about the nineteenth of July, when the Dog-Star rises before dawn. Ceos, like all the Cyclades, depends wholly upon their coming.

The story of Icarius is closely linked with the cult of Dionysus. Like Dionysus himself, who in one story was torn to pieces by the Titans and then restored to life, Icarius stands for the grape, which must perish if wine is to come into being. Eratosthenes linked with the legend a theory of the origins of drama, an art which had Dionysus as its patron, as well as the origins of the whole group of constellations which he connected with Icarius, Erigone and their possessions.

Many other identifications of the Maiden have been put forward. Some take her to be Demeter, the Corn-Goddess, or her daughter, Persephone: others think she is the Babylonian goddess Ishtar, the Egyptian Isis or the Syrian Atargatis; others make out that she is Fortune. But the two best-known identifications are the two put forward during the third century B.C. by two famous poets of the Hellenistic Age.

Virgo is a mutable and earthy sign, ruled by Mercury. Virgo types are intelligent, precise and often fussy; they are critics and craftsmen, not creators or commanders. Virgo is the patron sign of cats.

VII. Libra

The Scales   September 24 to October 23

The constellation called the Scales lies between Spica and Antares, the brightest star of Scorpio, and itself has no particularly bright star. This name seems not to occur before the second century B.C., although the 'horn' of the Scorpion is called 'scales' in an early Babylonian text; it looks as though the astrologers were responsible for its general adoption. Originally this space was filled by Chelae, the Claws of the Scorpion.

Some say that the name originated because of the scales used by the Egyptian god Osiris to weigh the souls of the dead; this is possible, but far from certain. The statement that the sign was called after one Mochos, a man of great clemency and justice, is absurd; the right reading of the name is Mouchos, and it obviously comes from an abbreviation of the Greek word Stathmouchos, 'the man who holds the balance'. Since the scales are unique in being not a person or an animal, but an object, many authors bring in a man who holds the scales. Some identified the Scales with Julius Caesar, also praised for clemency and justice. A comet which appeared during the games held in Caesar's honour in July of 44 B.C., four months after his murder, was claimed to have been his spirit, now exalted to the heavens; Ovid described how Caesar became incandescent as he flew through the sky; and Propertius makes him watch Augustus' victory at Actium from his place among the stars. To place Caesar in the Zodiac was a variation of the same idea. Virgil in the prelude to the first book of his *Georgics*, published in 29 B.C., asks Augustus whether he intends to join the slowly moving months as a new star, where a space lies open between Erigone (= Virgo) and the Claws; the Scorpion, he adds, voluntarily draws in his arms so as to leave Augustus a larger portion of the sky than a Zodiac sign normally occupies. But neither identification became popular; and the Scales are less often explained mythologically than any other sign of the Zodiac. The likeliest explanation of the name's origin seems to be that the scales symbolised the equal length of nights and days at the autumnal equinox that falls while the Sun is in the sign, a theory that fits well with the notion that it was the astrologers who made the name popular.

Myths of the Zodiac

Libra is an airy sign, ruled by Venus and tending towards harmony. Libra types are gentle, tolerant and diplomatic; Erasmus is a characteristic example.

VIII. Scorpio (or Scorpius)

The Scorpion   October 24 to November 22

Scorpio is a splendid constellation; it is too far south to be seen easily in England, but its brightest star, Antares, can be seen during the summer, lying right opposite Aldebaran and conspicuous by its red colour. The Egyptians found a scorpion, identified with the goddess Selk, among the stars, but it was not our scorpion. But the Babylonians identified it with this, and the Greeks mention it as early as the late sixth century.

The scorpion is commonly connected with the giant Orion, whose splendid constellation stands far away, for good reason. In one of his legends Orion figures as a Boeotian local hero, connected with the town of Hyria. In the days when the gods used to wander over the earth disguised as mortals, three strangers knocked at the door of Hyrieus, the local hero of this place, and asked for shelter. Hyrieus entertained them generously, slaughtering an ox to give them meat. These strangers were in fact the gods Zeus, Poseidon and Hermes. Having learned that their kind host, like all childless Greeks, greatly desired to have a son, they urinated into the hide of the ox and told him to bury it in the ground. After nine months a gigantic infant pushed its way up; the child was called Orion, a name somewhat resembling the Greek word for 'urine'. This legend has the hallmark of extreme antiquity.

Orion is always imagined as a great hunter; in the *Odyssey* Odysseus sees him in Hades, hunting again in death the beasts which he has slain in life. Sometimes he was imagined as hunting in the sky the Pleiades, whose name means 'doves'. His splendid constellation, with two great stars, the almost white Rigel and the orange-red Betelgueux, is conspicuous in the sky.

One group of legends connects Orion with Crete and other Aegean islands; these tend to make him a son of Poseidon by Euryale, daughter of the great Cretan monarch Minos. Some say that he could walk upon the water; others that he was so tall that while he walked upon the sea-bed his head projected above the waves.

One day Orion came to Chios, then ruled by Oenopion. Oenopion was a son of Dionysus, and his name comes from *oinos*, the word for wine; in those times wine was the main product of that fertile island. Somehow or other,

Myths of the Zodiac

Orion made himself a nuisance to his host. Some say that he was an unwelcome suitor of the king's daughter, Merope, others that he actually offered her violence; there is also a story that the king's wife was the object of his unwelcome attentions. Oenopion dealt with his formidable visitor very much as Odysseus dealt with the Cyclops, Polyphemus; he got him very drunk and then put his eyes out. Waking at a desolate spot on the sea shore and finding himself blind, Orion managed to make his way to a blacksmith's forge. There he carried off a boy called Cedalion, set him on his shoulders and made him guide him in the direction of the rising sun. The moment the sun's rays shone upon the face of the blind giant, he recovered his sight, and hurried off to take revenge upon Oenopion. In the nick of time Oenopion was saved by the god Poseidon, who guided him to a subterranean chamber where he was able to hide from his pursuer.

Most authorities connect Orion's death with the virgin goddess Artemis. Homer says that he was carried off by the goddess of the Dawn on account of his surpassing beauty, and that the gods resented her having taken a mortal lover and sent Artemis to kill him with her arrows. Other authors say that Orion tried to rape Artemis, and was killed by her in consequence. But in some versions their relations had not always been unfriendly. Aratus says that they were hunting together on Chios when Orion made his attempt; Istros, a writer of the second century B.C., even says that Artemis was in love with Orion and wished to marry him, and that Apollo killed him because he did not want to have him for a brother-in-law. Only a writer of the Hellenistic Age would have imagined Artemis as thinking for one moment of renouncing her virginity.

As early as the astronomical poem ascribed to Hesiod, Orion is said to have died from being bitten by a scorpion. This story obviously owes its origin to the presence of the scorpion in the sky, who even in Homer figures as a constellation. While hunting in Crete with Artemis and her mother Leto—Artemis might hunt with male persons, as she did with Hippolytus, without entering into any erotic relations with them—Orion boasted that he would kill every wild beast upon the earth. Angry at these words, the Earth sent up a giant scorpion, which slew him with its bite. The Scorpion is the only sign of the Zodiac whose myth originated as a star-myth.

Scorpio is fixed and watery; it is ruled by Mars. Being the eighth sign, it is sometimes related to the eighth of the astrological houses, which is the

Scorpio

house of death (see p. 22). Scorpio types are tough, aggressive, amorous; though they are often sinister, they may be good company. Goering is an instance of this; other Scorpio characters are Nelson, Goethe and Nietzsche.

IX. Sagittarius

The Archer   November 23 to December 21

East of the bright star Antares in Scorpio we may find Sagittarius, the most southerly of the Zodiacal constellations; none of its stars is brighter than the average. The name of Archer goes back to Babylonian astronomy; figures resembling this Archer were used in Babylonia as boundary stones.

The Greeks identified the Archer either with a Centaur or with a Satyr, or Silen. Centaurs have a human trunk rising out of a horse's body; Silens have the ears, tails and hooves of horses, but are otherwise like humans. The kind of satyr that is goatish rather than equine appears only during the Hellenistic age; classical satyrs belong to the horse type.

Centaurs and Satyrs were violent and lascivious. Satyrs despite their bravado were weak and cowardly, but Centaurs were formidable fighters, who would gallop down the slopes of Mount Pelion, in Thessaly, their principal abode, brandishing the young pine trees which they uprooted to use as weapons and spreading terror over the countryside.

Centaurs owed their origin to the misdemeanours of the Thessalian hero Ixion. He is said to have been the first mortal to commit murder. Having quarrelled with his father-in-law over the amount of his wife's dowry, Ixion murdered him by causing him to fall into a concealed pit. Curiously enough Zeus instead of punishing him was somehow induced to purify him from the guilt of murder; one would dearly like to know how the tragic poet Aeschylus, who wrote a whole trilogy, now lost, about Ixion, justified this action. Ixion returned his kindness by having the impudence to plan to seduce Zeus' own consort, Hera. Hearing of his intentions, Zeus fashioned a cloud into an exact likeness of his wife; and from the union of this cloud, the Centaurs, all except one, who will be dealt with presently, were born. Then Ixion was bound to a wheel that eternally whirled round and placed in Tartarus as a warning to others; this is an unpleasant fate, yet one cannot help thinking that the trick with the cloud must have caused considerable pleasure for Ixion before he discovered his mistake. The story of the Centaurs' origin is one of the many myths based on the naive false etymologies that were so prevalent among the ancients, for the word *Centaur*

looks as if it might be formed from a word meaning 'poke' and a word meaning 'the breezes'.

It was unwise of the half-brother of the Centaurs, the great hero Pirithous (see p. 55) to invite these embarrassing relations to his wedding. They were not used to strong drink, and in consequence went berserk and tried to carry off the bride and other female guests present at the feast. The sculptures of the west pediment of the Temple of Zeus at Olympia (see p. 52) show the battle between the Centaurs and the heroes who sprang to the defence. The faces of the heroes and their women by convention remain impassive, but those of the monsters are distorted by rage and lust. In the centre, the presence of the towering figure of Apollo assures us that the monsters will finally be defeated.

Those Centaurs who escaped death on that occasion at the hands of Pirithous, his great friend Theseus and the other heroes who fought for the Lapiths, the people of that part of Thessaly, were driven from that country and spread over Greece. One of these stragglers, who was named Nessus, earned a living by ferrying travellers over a mountain torrent, the Evenus. One day Heracles hired him to carry over his newly-wed bride, Deianira; in mid-stream the Centaur was so foolish as to lay hands on her. A scream from Deianira, and the hero took his great bow and sent a poisoned arrow through the Centaur's side. As he lay dying, Nessus asked Deianira to accept the robe he wore in memory of him. She must store it carefully away, and if Heracles ever put it on, he would never love another woman. Years afterwards, when Heracles had stormed and sacked Oechalia for the love of its king's daughter Iole, Deianira remembered the Centaur's gift. As Heracles was sacrificing on the top of a high mountain, Mount Oeta, in north-eastern Greece, not far from Thermopylae, the herald Lichas brought him his wife's splendid gift. Heracles put on the robe, and at once it clung to his body and began to burn away the flesh; the deadly poison of the Hydra's blood, warmed by the sun, had become active. Then Heracles remembered a prophecy that he should die at the hand of one already dead. His father had told him that when the time came for him to die, he should order a great pyre to be prepared, have his body placed upon it and cause the pyre to be ignited. His son Hyllus refused to obey so fearful a command; a passing hero, Philoctetes, lit the pyre for Heracles, and received the legacy of his great bow in consequence. The pyre blazed up, and consumed the mortal part of

Sagittarius

Heracles. But Zeus caught the great hero's spirit in his arms and carried it, now made immortal, to Olympus, where even Hera accepted Heracles as a god and in token of reconciliation gave him the hand in marriage of her daughter Hebe, goddess of youth.

The Archer in the sky is most often identified with the one Centaur who was not a son of Ixion and the cloud, and whose character was wholly unlike that of those who were. This is the noble Centaur, Chiron. True, the identification first appears comparatively late, perhaps not before Cicero's contemporary, the learned Roman astrologer Nigidius Figulus; but from that time it became popular. Kronos, father of Zeus and ruler of the universe before him, pursued Philyra, nymph of the linden tree. To escape him she took the form of a mare, and Kronos came after her in that of a stallion. That is how their offspring came to have the shape of a Centaur, combined with a nature very different from that of other Centaurs.

Like the other Centaurs, Chiron lived on Mount Pelion; but unlike them he led a tranquil domestic existence in his cave together with his mother Philyra and his wife Chariclo. He played an important part in one of the most famous unions of mythology, that between the sea-nymph Thetis and the great hero Peleus. The beauty of Thetis had nearly caused a battle between Zeus and his brother Poseidon, and had this union with Thetis taken place would have led to the fall of Zeus from power. Poseidon was ready to fight his brother for the sake of Thetis; but worse danger was threatened by the prophecy that Thetis was destined to have a son mightier than his father. The only person who knew the secret was a deadly enemy of Zeus, the Titan Prometheus. To punish him for having given fire to men, Zeus had kept Prometheus prisoner for countless ages with unspeakable torments. But Zeus' son Heracles visited the desolate spot where Prometheus was fastened, wishing to inquire the way to the far west, where he had to perform one of his labours. Through Heracles' good offices, Zeus and Prometheus struck a bargain; in return for his release, Prometheus revealed the secret.

The gods now realised that it was not safe to allow Thetis to mate with Zeus, or with any of his brothers. She must be handed over to a mortal, so that her son would be a mortal too. But this was not easy to effect, for Thetis like other marine divinities had the power of taking any shape she pleased, and even a god would have found it hard to catch her. The mortal chosen by Zeus to be her bridegroom was Peleus, who as a son of Aeacus was a grandson of Zeus himself. Zeus also wished to reward him for his virtue; tempted as Joseph was by the wife of Potiphar by Hippolyta, wife of his host, the Thessalian king Acastus, Peleus had held out against her blandishments. Exposed upon Mount Pelion without weapons through the machinations of the scorned fury, Peleus was saved by Chiron's giving him a knife with which he could protect himself. Either by his wise counsel or with his magic herbs, Chiron at the command of Zeus was able to help Peleus to win Thetis. Lying in wait for her when she came by night to a deserted beach, Peleus clasped her in his arms. Chiron had warned him that through all her transformations he must hold her fast; and though she took the shape of a serpent, of a lion, and of blazing fire Peleus did not let go. Her son by Peleus was Achilles, mightier not only than Peleus but than all heroes of the generations after Heracles.

Some say that Thetis accompanied Peleus to his Thessalian palace, but she was not well suited to domestic life. One night Peleus found her holding the infant Achilles over a fire. Thetis was simply applying the approved technique for making the child immortal, which consisted in burning away his mortal part, as the mortal part of Heracles was burned away by the pyre on Oeta (see p. 82). Furious at being interrupted, Thetis flung down the infant and vanished to the depths of the sea, never to return. Unable to bring up Achilles by himself, Peleus confided him to Chiron, who, in his cave on Mount Pelion taught him not only hunting and fighting, but the use of healing herbs and the music with which he solaced his idleness during his absence from the field of battle before Troy. The young Achilles used his great swiftness of foot to track down animals and eat them raw, thus developing his mighty strength. Now other young heroes were brought by their fathers to be trained by Chiron, who became the Dr. Busby of the Greek heroic world. Fearing his brother Pelias (see p. 33) Aeson brought his son Jason; some say that Anchises brought Aeneas, his son by the goddess Aphrodite, the fierce Aetolian hero Tydeus his son Diomedes, and Apollo his son by the nymph Cyllene, Aristaeus (see p. 72); in defiance of mythological chronology, some even added Heracles to this list of pupils.

Heracles was a friend of Chiron, and plays a part in the sad story of his end. He had been a guest at the wedding of Pirithous, and greatly contributed to the destruction of the Centaurs. After the battle, Chiron entertained him in his cave, and while idly playing with his guest's quiver had the misfortune to

84

Sagittarius

drop an arrow so that it grazed his foot. The Hydra's poison (see p. 60) caused him grievous agony; Chiron as the son of Kronos by a nymph was an immortal, but now he wished for death. Luckily, a means by which he might obtain it was at hand. Heracles had lately helped Zeus to make his agreement with Prometheus; but Zeus had earlier declared that Prometheus could never be released until an immortal was willing to give up his immortality and take the place in Tartarus that had been allotted to Prometheus. Glad to escape from his perpetual torment, Chiron renounced his immortality, and Prometheus could be let go. Aeschylus seems to have invented this legend for the purpose of his trilogy about Prometheus; it does not fit easily with the chronology of Chiron's part in the affairs of Peleus and Thetis.

The less common representation of the Archer as a Silen was put to a strange use by a minor tragedian of the Hellenistic age, Sosibius. He related that the nine Muses in their Boeotian home upon Mount Helicon made a favourite of their nurse's son. The nurse was called Eupheme, which means 'good utterance' or 'reverend utterance'; reverend utterance implied avoiding words of ill omen, and so could have the meaning 'silence'. The son was called Krotos, which means 'clapping', and so can mean 'applause'. This Krotos was the inventor of the bow, and often used it from a horse; he both entertained the Muses with his archery and equitation and applauded when they displayed their arts. To reward him, they asked Zeus to translate him to the heavens.

Since he was a rider, Zeus gave him horse's feet; since he was an archer, he gave him a bow; since the Muses like Dionysus took delight in satyrs, he gave him a satyr's tail. This curious flight of fancy could have been made only during the Hellenistic age, and by one of its less distinguished poets.

Sagittarius is ruled by Jupiter. Half man and half beast, he has a dual nature; aiming at a lofty target, he still keeps his feet on the ground. He is fiery, but with a purifying fire, like the fire at the heart of the flame; it may burn for spiritual or intellectual objects. Sagittarius types are explorers, adventurers, pioneers; strong and decided, they tend to throw their weight about. Beethoven, Lincoln and Churchill are among them.

X. Capricorn

The Goat   December 22 to January 20

Three stars in the head of Aquila, the Eagle, point towards the tail of the Goat, who lies between the star Altair in the Eagle and the star of the first magnitude, Fomalhaut, in the southern Fish. The origins of Capricorn may be Egyptian, but he was known to the Babylonians from early times. His Babylonian name was also the name of a kind of fish, and he is often depicted with a fish's tail. His stars are faint, except two double ones in the upper right-hand corner. As the sign of the winter solstice Capricorn has special importance; under him falls the birthday of the Unconquerable Sun on 25 December, later the birthday of Christ.

Epimenides, the Cretan poet and medicine man of the sixth century B.C.—the person who presented logicians with a famous puzzle by saying that all Cretans were liars—seems to have made Aigokeros ('Goat-horn', the Greek name of Capricorn) the son of Aigipan, 'Goat-Pan'. Aigipan is the same as Pan, the god who had the feet and legs of a goat.

Many different stories of Pan's origin are told. Usually Hermes figures as his father; Hermes, as the god of cunning, the patron of traders and a lover of the opposite sex is an appropriate parent for him. Also, Hermes was born in Arcadia, the most mountainous country in all Greece, in a cave on the slopes of Mount Cyllene; and Pan's worship seems to have started in Arcadia, where he was a god of shepherds and the inventor of the shepherd's pipe.

Some say that his mother was a Nymph called Callisto, 'the beautiful one'; Pan is regularly worshipped together with the Nymphs, sharing the shrines that were constructed beside springs of water, sacred to them. But many authors say that his mother was the supposedly chaste wife of Odysseus, Penelope, either by Hermes or Apollo or through the combined operations of the many suitors who importuned Penelope during the long absence of her husband (without success, if we may believe the author of the *Odyssey*). Such paternity would certainly account for Pan's goatish appearance and the goatish element in his nature.

He is imagined as a genial god, friendly to men and constantly pursuing the Nymphs who are his companions. But he had also a more sinister side to

him. He was dangerous to encounter in the mid-day heat, for he was capable of fierce rages, and he had the power to strike blind terror into men, sometimes causing whole armies to 'panic', as we still say.

In 490 B.C., after the Athenians had won a brilliant victory over a Persian punitive expedition at Marathon, on the east coast of Attica, the news of the battle was brought to Athens by a special messenger, called Philippides, an athlete who had trained himself to compete in the long-distance race at the great games of Greece. While Philippides was on his way he heard a voice calling him by name. It was Pan, who claimed a share in the Athenian victory, and complained that the Athenians did him no honour. When Philippides arrived in Athens, he reported his experience, and a state cult of Pan was immediately set up; every year he was to receive sacrifices and be honoured by a torch-race. From that time, his worship spread widely over Greek territories.

Plutarch in his treatise on the decline of the Greek oracles reports that during the reign of Tiberius (A.D. 14–37) an Egyptian sailor named Thamous was steering his ship towards Italy when in the neighbourhood of the island of Paxos he heard a voice call him three times. When he answered, the voice told him that when he arrived at Palodes (a place of which we have no other knowledge), he was to announce that the great Pan was dead. Thamous decided that if the ship sailed straight past the place in question, he would do nothing, but if there was no wind and the ship moved slowly he would comply with the command. As it happened there was no wind when the ship arrived there, and Thamous shouted out the message; from the shore came a loud groan, as of many voices. When the ship came to Rome the story got about, and Thamous was summoned by the Emperor. Tiberius consulted his learned friends as to who might be meant by 'the great Pan', and they advised him that it was the son of Hermes and Penelope.

Tiberius was Emperor at the time of the crucifixion of Christ, and not surprisingly this story aroused great interest among Christians. Plutarch tells the story as evidence that 'daimones', or inferior divinities, live a long time but are not immortal. The bishop Eusebius, who lived in the fourth century A.D., under Constantine the Great, thought that Pan and all other 'daimones' were driven from the world by Christ; for him 'daimon' already meant almost what we mean by 'demon'. It is quite probable that the devil derived his attributes of horns and tail from Pan in consequence of this story. Others

Capricorn

thought that the great Pan whose death was reported was none other than Christ himself. These people were no doubt influenced by the knowledge that the word *pan* in Greek means 'all', a circumstance which led many allegorists to make Pan into a god of all things, a fancy that seems not to be attested earlier than the time of Nero.

But to return to Aigokeros, or Capricorn, according to Epimenides his mother was Amaltheia, the divine goat who suckled the infant Zeus. Determined to save Zeus from being swallowed, like all her other children, by her husband Kronos, jealous of his power, Rhea smuggled away Zeus as soon as he was born to Crete, where in the solitude of a cave high on Mount Dicte Amaltheia nursed him. One of her horns became the miraculous horn of plenty, the Cornucopia.

Aigokeros was imagined, like his father, as being half man and half goat in shape; often he has a fish's tail. When the gods were fighting to defend their power against their formidable enemies, the Titans, he made a trumpet out of a conch-shell. The Titans were suddenly terrified by a tremendous blast; they fled in panic. To reward him Aigokeros was given a fish's tail as a memento of the incident; it was suggestive of the sea, from which the shell had come.

Often Capricorn is made identical with Pan himself. When the gods in terror of the huge monster Typhon took animal shape, Pan took the form of a goat. That legend was invented to account for the animal shapes of so many Egyptian gods, and later made use of to explain that attributed to Pan. The strange form of Capricorn, obviously of oriental origin, clearly puzzled the Greeks. Some of them replaced him by a sea-nymph, one of the countless daughters of the sea-god Nereus.

Capricorn is an earthy sign, ruled by Saturn. Those born under it are subtle, calm, collected, gay and witty and yet melancholy. People who look like goats or fish are often Capricorn types; they tend to become obsessed with a single notion, such as state-worship or religious mania. Joan of Arc and Albert Schweitzer belonged to Capricorn, and so did Woodrow Wilson.

XI. Aquarius

The Water-Pourer   January 21 to February 19

Two stars in the square of Pegasus act as pointers to the Water-Pourer, an obscure group of stars spread over a wide area; only one of them is even of the third magnitude. Two jets of water flow from the urn, or hydria, carried by the Water-Pourer in the direction of the Southern Fish.

It seems that the Water-Pourer was first the god of the Nile, on whom the life of Egypt depended, and later a female Babylonian water divinity. Usually he is shown standing as he pours out his water; but sometimes he is presented, as here, in the attitude often displayed by Greek statues of river-gods. On the pediment of the temple of Zeus at Olympia, the two local river-gods Cladeus and Alpheus are so presented. The Greek name for Aquarius—Hydrochous—could be applied to a vessel as easily as to a person, and a few monuments show simply a vessel with no person to hold it.

The Water-Pourer could be most easily accommodated in Greek myth if he became a cup-bearer. The cup-bearer of the gods was Ganymedes, or Ganymede. This beautiful boy was the son of a king of Troy; if his father was Tros, then Ganymede was Priam's uncle; if it was Laomedon, he was Priam's brother. Two great kings, Tantalus and Minos, are said to have pursued him; but it was the divine father of these kings, Zeus himself, who won the prize. Zeus sent his messenger, the eagle, to carry the boy up to Olympus, where he was made immortal and served the gods as cupbearer. In return, his father received a rich reward; he was given a stock of miraculously swift horses, sired by the North Wind himself. Laomedon, a notoriously shifty character, hired the gods Poseidon and Apollo to build the walls of Troy, only to cheat them of their agreed reward. To punish him Poseidon sent a terrible sea-monster; Laomedon learned that it would go away only if his own daughter, the beautiful Hesione, was handed over to it to be devoured. Only one living person could be of use to Laomedon in this situation, and that was Heracles, who conveniently happened to be at hand. He tackled the monster, and by a most cunning method; he simply allowed the beast to swallow him, and then cut his way out of its inside. But when he claimed his agreed reward, which was the possession of the horses,

Laomedon once more cheated. This brought disaster to the Trojans; for Heracles brought an army to Troy and took and sacked the city. His partner in the assault was the great hero Telamon, himself a grandson of Zeus. Hesione was handed over to Telamon as a concubine, and by him had a son, the great archer Teucer; by his legitimate wife, Eriboea, Telamon was father of the mighty Ajax.

In a famous chorus of his play *The Trojan Women*, Euripides makes his chorus of Trojan female prisoners after their city's second sack by the Greeks under Agamemnon dwell poignantly on the contrast between the eternal happiness of the beautiful boy living for ever on Olympus and the stark misery to which his family and his city have finally been brought.

Inn signs bearing the Eagle and Child preserve a memory of Ganymedes; so does the word *catamite*, which comes from a Latin corruption of his name.

We have seen that for the Babylonians the Water-Pourer was a female figure. Consistently with this, some people identified the constellation with another person said to have served the gods as cup-bearer. This is Hebe, daughter of Hera and goddess of youth. When after all his labours Heracles finally ended his life on earth and became immortal, Hera, who had been from the start his jealous enemy, had to accept him as a god and a fellow-inmate of Olympus. In token of their reconciliation, she gave him as his bride her beautiful daughter Hebe. Heracles' possession of the goddess of youth was another token of his victory in the struggle against death that seems from the earliest times to have been a central feature of his legend.

A third identification of the Water-Pourer is with Deucalion, the Greek equivalent of Noah. Legends of a mighty deluge which once destroyed all or nearly all the human race seem to have spread from Mesopotamia, the land of great rivers, over all the surrounding territories. The Greeks had a story that at one time Zeus became so enraged by the misdeeds of men that he sent floods which eliminated all of them, except Deucalion and his wife Pyrrha. Zeus finally decided to repopulate the earth, and did so by causing Deucalion and Pyrrha to collect stones and drop them as they walked along. These stones turned into men; the story plays upon the likeness between *laos*, meaning 'people', and *laas* (less often *laos*), meaning 'stone'. It was presumably because of his connection with the great flood that Deucalion figured as the Water-Pourer; but the identification is a late one, not found before the last century before Christ.

Aquarius

This was not the only occasion on which Zeus thought of sending a great flood to punish men. A similar story was told in the *Cypria*, an early Greek epic which told the story of the Trojan War up to the point at which the *Iliad* begins. This started by telling how Zeus informed the gods in council that he was thinking of doing the same thing again. Luckily for mankind, Zeus encountered criticism, as usual, from Momus, the god of fault-finding. 'Why go to all the trouble of arranging for a flood?', said he, 'if I were you, I should go down to earth, find an attractive woman and beget a beautiful daughter. Men will fight wars over her, and so reduce their own numbers without your having to bother to do it for them'. Zeus took his advice and transformed himself into a swan and Hermes, his usual companion on such expeditions, into a falcon. While Leda, the beautiful queen of Sparta, was bathing in a river, the swan, pursued by the falcon, took refuge in her arms. In consequence, Leda laid the famous eggs (see p. 53).

Aquarius is a fixed and airy sign, ruled by Saturn. Aquarius types lack respect for traditions and conventions, which may make them democrats, but may also make them innovators. They are intelligent and independent in their thinking; but they are sometimes tactless, stubborn, or even fanatical.

XII. Pisces

The Fishes   February 20 to March 20

This line of obscure stars runs beneath the Great Square of Pegasus; after Cancer they are the faintest of the Zodiacal constellations. The Northern Fish can be made out just south of Andromeda's hip; the Southern (or Western) Fish lies south of the Great Square. The tails of the Fishes are tied together by a chain, lying between the brighter of Andromeda's feet and the head of Aries.

The Fishes existed in early Egypt, and then in Babylon; they belong to Babylonian mythology, and are the only Signs the Greeks failed to explain with one of their own myths. Their myth pertains to the Syrian goddess Derceto or Atargatis, whom the Greeks identified with Aphrodite. Two fishes found in the Euphrates a giant egg, which they propelled to land; there a dove settled upon it. From this egg after a few days there emerged the Syrian Goddess; at her request the great god honoured the fishes by placing them in the heavens. According to another Syrian tale, Derceto once fell into a pond and was rescued by a fish.

The Greeks of the Hellenistic age provided the Fishes with a myth with rather more Hellenic colouring by using the story that the gods all changed their shape in order to hide from the dreadful monster Typhon. This tale was invented in order to explain why many of the gods of Egypt had the shapes of animals (see p. 42). On that occasion, Aphrodite and her son Eros, the love-god, dived into the Euphrates. To do this they took the shape of fish; or as another version has it they were rescued by fish, who were rewarded for their kindness by a place in the sky. So that they should not be separated, they tied their tails together. This story is a curious mixture of Syrian, Egyptian and Greek mythology.

Pisces is a mutable and watery sign, ruled by Jupiter. Pisces types are gentle, shy and sensitive; at best, they are idealists, at worst drifters. Hölderlin and Nijinsky belonged to Pisces; but so did some tougher characters, including Schopenhauer.

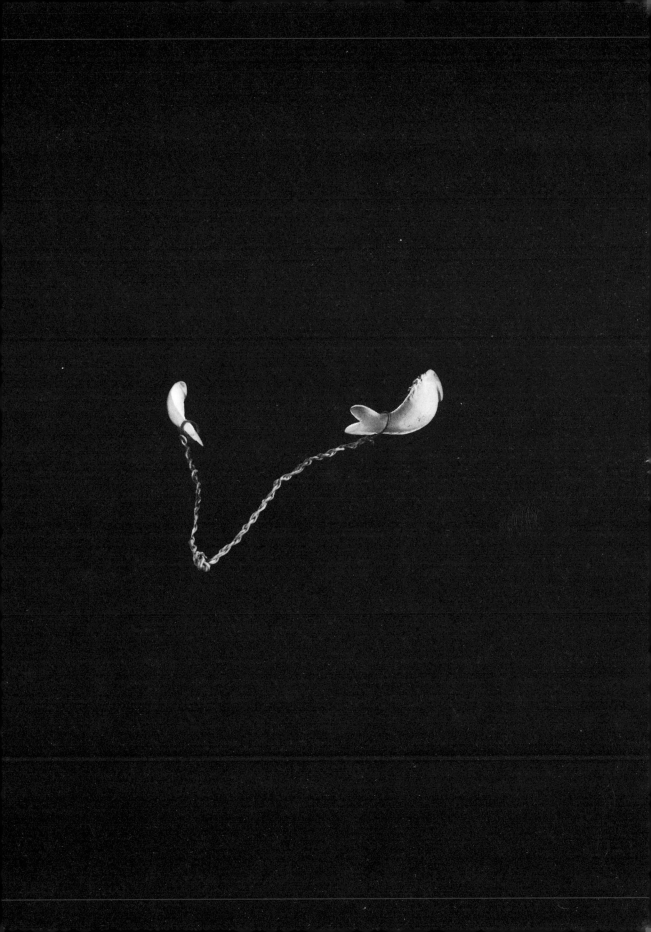